A Gift For

From

Date

THE GREATEST BIBLE PROMISES

FOR THE ANOINTING OF THE HOLY SPIRIT

SMITH WIGGLESWORTH

WHITAKER
HOUSE

Greatest Bible Promises for
the Anointing of the Holy Spirit

ISBN: 978-1-62911-869-7
eBook ISBN: 978-1-62911-872-7
Printed in the United States of America
© 2017 by Whitaker House

Whitaker House
1030 Hunt Valley Circle
New Kensington, PA 15068
www.whitakerhouse.com

Library of Congress Cataloging-in-Publication Data (Pending)

1 2 3 4 5 6 7 8 9 10 11 ᘈ 24 23 22 21 20 19 18 17

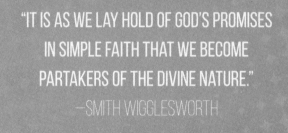

"IT IS AS WE LAY HOLD OF GOD'S PROMISES
IN SIMPLE FAITH THAT WE BECOME
PARTAKERS OF THE DIVINE NATURE."
—SMITH WIGGLESWORTH

CONTENTS

CHAPTER FOUR: THE GIFTS OF THE SPIRIT

CHAPTER FIVE: POWER OF THE HOLY SPIRIT

CHAPTER SIX: GOING DEEPER

CHAPTER SEVEN: A SPIRIT-LED LIFE

A WORD FROM THE EDITOR

The Greatest Bible Promises is a collection of God's promises in Scripture, from the *King James Version Easy Read Bible* (KJVER), combined with beloved quotes from the various writings of the Apostle of Faith, Smith Wigglesworth (1859–1947).

An encounter with Smith Wigglesworth was an unforgettable experience. This seems to be the universal reaction of all who knew him or heard him speak. Wigglesworth was a simple yet remarkable man who was used by God in extraordinary ways. He had a contagious and inspiring faith. Under his ministry, thousands of people came to salvation, committed themselves to a deeper faith in Christ, received the baptism in the Holy Spirit, and were miraculously healed. The power that brought these kinds of results was the presence of the Holy Spirit, who filled Smith Wigglesworth and used him in bringing the good news of the gospel to people all over the world. Wigglesworth gave glory to God for everything that was accomplished through his ministry, and he wanted people to understand his work only in this context, because his sole desire was that people would see Jesus and not himself.

It is our hope that by reading Wigglesworth's words of wisdom and inspiration combined with the wonderful promises found in Scripture, you will truly experience the divine presence of our miraculous God and take to heart one of Wigglesworth's favorite sayings: "Only believe!"

LET ME SAY A WORD TO YOUR HEARTS...

But the Comforter, which is the Holy Ghost, whom the Father will send in My name, He shall teach you all things, and bring all things to your remembrance, whatsoever I have said to you.
—John 14:26

Most of us here today are diligently seeking God's best. We feel that we would pay any price for His best. God knows my heart. I do not have an atom of desire outside the perfect will of God, and God knows this. But Wigglesworth, like everybody else, occasionally has to ask, "What is wrong with me? I do not feel the anointing," and if there is anything to repent of, I get right down before God and get it out. You cannot cover over sins; you cannot cover over faults. You must get to the bottom of them. I cannot have the anointing, the power of the Holy Spirit, the life of Christ, and the manifest glory except through self-abasement and complete renunciation of self—with God alone enthroned and Wigglesworth dead to himself. It must be of God, and if a person will only examine the conditions and act upon them, I tell you, things will come off wonderfully.

～

It is the Spirit who gives liberty. The prophet is nothing, but the Spirit brings us into attainment where we sit at His feet and seek with Him and have communications of things divine. For now we are not belonging to the earth; we are "transformed by the renewing of our mind" and "set in heavenly places with Christ Jesus." You must cease to be. That is a difficult thing—for both you and me—but it is no trouble at all when you are in the hands of the Potter. You are only wrong when you are kicking. You are all right when you are still and He is forming you afresh. So let Him form you afresh today into a new vessel so that you will stand the stress.

～

God wants to promote us. He wants us to get away from our own thoughts and our own foolishness, and get to a definite place, believing that He exists and that "He is a rewarder of those who diligently seek Him." Have you gotten to the place where you dare to do this?

～

Have you gotten to the place where you are no longer going to murmur when you are undergoing a trial? Are you going to go around weeping, telling people about it, or are you going to say, "Thank you, Lord, for putting me on the top"?

~

I believe God wants us to know more about the baptism of the Holy Spirit. And I believe that God wants us to know the truth in such a way that we may all have a clear understanding of what He means when He desires all His people to receive the Holy Spirit. There is a life in the Spirit that makes you free, and there is an audacity about it, and there is a personality in it—it is God in you. God is able to so transform you and change you that all the old order has to go before God's new order. Do you think that God will make you to be a failure? God never made man to be a failure. He made man to be a son, to walk the earth in the power of the Spirit, to be master over the flesh and the Devil, until nothing arises within him except what will magnify and glorify the Lord.

~

Enter into the promises of God. It is your inheritance. You will do more in one year if you are really filled with the Holy Spirit than you could do in fifty years apart from Him. I pray that you may be so filled with Him that it will not be possible for you to move without a revival of some kind resulting.

—*Smith Wigglesworth*

"IT IS IMPORTANT THAT WE KNOW WE CAN DO NOTHING IN OURSELVES. HOWEVER, WE MAY KNOW THAT WE ARE CLOTHED WITH THE POWER OF GOD SO THAT, IN A SENSE, WE ARE NOT IN THE NATURAL MAN. AS WE GO FORTH IN THIS POWER, THINGS WILL TAKE PLACE AS THEY TOOK PLACE IN THE DAYS OF THE DISCIPLES."

—SMITH WIGGLESWORTH

1

THE COMFORTER

THE PERSON OF THE HOLY SPIRIT

And the earth was without form, and void; and darkness was upon the face of the deep. And the Spirit of God moved upon the face of the waters.   GENESIS 1:2

And the LORD said, My Spirit shall not always strive with man, for that he also is flesh: yet his days shall be a hundred and twenty years.   GENESIS 6:3

But there remained two of the men in the camp, the name of the one was Eldad, and the name of the other Medad: and the spirit rested upon them; and they were of them that were written, but went not out to the tabernacle: and they prophesied in the camp.   NUMBERS 11:26

You gave also Your good Spirit to instruct them, and withheld not Your manna from their mouth, and gave them water for their thirst.   NEHEMIAH 9:20

By His spirit He has garnished the heavens; His hand has formed the crooked serpent.　　　　　JOB 26:13

The spirit of God has made me, and the breath of the Almighty has given me life.　　　　　JOB 33:4

Cast me not away from Your presence; and take not Your Holy Spirit from me.　　　　　PSALM 51:11

Where shall I go from Your spirit? or where shall I flee from Your presence?　　　　　PSALM 139:7

You send forth Your spirit, they are created: and You renew the face of the earth.　　　　　PSALM 104:30

Turn you at my reproof: behold, I will pour out my spirit to you, I will make known my words to you.　　　　　PROVERBS 1:23

The fear of the LORD is the beginning of wisdom: and the knowledge of the holy is understanding.　　　　　PROVERBS 9:10

I, even I, am the LORD; and beside Me there is no savior. I have declared, and have saved, and I have showed, when there was no strange god among you: therefore you are My witnesses, says the LORD, that I am God. Yea, before the day was I am He; and there is none that can deliver out of My hand: I will work, and who shall let it?　　　　　ISAIAH 43:11–13

So shall they fear the name of the LORD from the west, and His glory from the rising of the sun. When the enemy shall come in like a flood, the Spirit of the LORD shall lift up a standard against him. ISAIAH 59:19

As for Me, this is My covenant with them, says the LORD; My spirit that is upon you, and My words which I have put in your mouth, shall not depart out of your mouth, nor out of the mouth of your seed, nor out of the mouth of your seed's seed, says the LORD, from hereafter and for ever. ISAIAH 59:21

But they rebelled, and vexed His holy Spirit: therefore He was turned to be their enemy, and He fought against them. ISAIAH 63:10

A new heart also will I give you, and a new Spirit will I put within you: and I will take away the stony heart out of your flesh, and I will give you a heart of flesh. And I will put My Spirit within you, and cause you to walk in My statutes, and you shall keep My judgments, and do them. EZEKIEL 36:26–27

INSIGHTS ON FAITH FROM SMITH WIGGLESWORTH

What an inspiration it is to give God the supreme place in our lives! When we do, He will so fill us with the Holy Spirit that the government will rest upon His shoulders. (See Isaiah 9:6.) I hope that we will believe and come into the holy realm of the knowledge of what it means to yield our all to God. Just think of what would happen if we only dared to believe God!

⌒

Then right through you will come forth a river of divine anointing that will sustain you in the bitterest place. It will give life to the deadest formality and say to the weak, "Be strong," and to them who have no might, "The Lord of Hosts is here to comfort you." God wants us to be like the rising of the sun, filled with the rays of heaven, all the time beaming forth the gladness of the Spirit of the Almighty. Possibility is the greatest thing of your life.

⌒

God wants to show you that there is a place where we can live in the Spirit and not be subject to the flesh. We can live in the Spirit until sin has no dominion over us. We reign in life and see the covering of God over us in the Spirit.

THE PERSON OF THE HOLY SPIRIT

I indeed baptize you with water to repentance. but He that comes after me is mightier than I, whose shoes I am not worthy to bear: He shall baptize you with the Holy Ghost, and with fire: whose fan is in His hand, and He will thoroughly purge His floor, and gather His wheat into the garner; but He will burn up the chaff with unquenchable fire. MATTHEW 3:11–12

For it is not you that speak, but the Spirit of your Father which speaks in you. MATTHEW 10:20

But when they shall lead you, and deliver you up, take no thought beforehand what you shall speak, neither do you premeditate: but whatsoever shall be given you in that hour, that speak you: for it is not you that speak, but the Holy Ghost. MARK 13:11

Watch you and pray, lest you enter into temptation. The spirit truly is ready, but the flesh is weak. MARK 14:38

And the angel answered and said to her, The Holy Ghost shall come upon you, and the power of the Highest shall overshadow you: therefore also that holy thing which shall be born of you shall be called the Son of God. LUKE 1:35

And, behold, there was a man in Jerusalem, whose name was Simeon; and the same man was just and devout, waiting for the consolation of Israel: and the Holy Ghost was upon him.

LUKE 2:25

And Jesus being full of the Holy Ghost returned from Jordan, and was led by the Spirit into the wilderness.　　LUKE 4:1

Jesus answered, Verily, verily, I say to you, Except a man be born of water and of the Spirit, he cannot enter into the kingdom of God. That which is born of the flesh is flesh; and that which is born of the Spirit is spirit. Marvel not that I said to you, You must be born again. The wind blows where it lists, and you hear the sound thereof, but can not tell where it comes, and where it goes: so is every one that is born of the Spirit.　　JOHN 3:5–8

It is the spirit that quickens; the flesh profits nothing: the words that I speak to you, they are spirit, and they are life.　　JOHN 6:63

In the last day, that great day of the feast, Jesus stood and cried, saying, If any man thirst, let him come to Me, and drink. He that believes on Me, as the scripture has said, out of his belly shall flow rivers of living water. (But this spoke He of the Spirit, which they that believe on Him should receive: for the Holy Ghost was not yet given; because that Jesus was not yet glorified.)　　JOHN 7:37–39

If you love Me, keep My commandments. And I will pray the Father, and He shall give you another Comforter, that He may abide with you for ever; even the Spirit of truth; whom the world cannot receive, because it sees Him not, neither knows Him: but you know Him; for He dwells with you, and shall be in you.

JOHN 14:15–17

But when the Comforter is come, whom I will send to you from the Father, even the Spirit of truth, which proceeds from the Father, He shall testify of Me.

JOHN 15:26

I have yet many things to say to you, but you cannot bear them now. However when He, the Spirit of truth, is come, He will guide you into all truth: for He shall not speak of Himself; but whatsoever He shall hear, that shall He speak: and He will show you things to come. He shall glorify Me: for He shall receive of Mine, and shall show it to you. All things that the Father has are Mine: therefore said I, that He shall take of Mine, and shall show it to you.

JOHN 16:12–15

INSIGHTS ON FAITH FROM SMITH WIGGLESWORTH

So God the Holy Spirit would have us to understand that there is a place in the Holy Spirit where there is no condemnation. This place is holiness, purity, righteousness, higher ground, perfection, and being more perfected in the presence of God. This higher ground state is holy desire. It is perfection where God is bringing us to live in such a way that He may smile through us and act upon us until our bodies become a flame of light ignited by Omnipotence. This is God's plan for us in the inheritance. It is an inheritance in the race that God wants us in today. This race, this divine race, this crowned race, this divine place is for us today.

⌣

I am hungry that I may be more full, that God may choose me for His service. And I know that the greatest qualification is to be filled with the Spirit. The Holy Spirit has the divine commission from heaven to impart revelation to every son of God concerning the Lord Jesus, to unfold to us the gifts and the fruit of the Spirit. He will take of the things of Christ and show them to us.

⌣

Oh, the power of the Holy Spirit creates new men and new women. The Holy Spirit takes away your stony heart and gives you a heart of flesh.

THE PERSON OF THE HOLY SPIRIT

Then said Jesus to them again, Peace be to you: as My Father has sent Me, even so send I you. And when He had said this, He breathed on them, and says to them, Receive you the Holy Ghost: Whosoever sins you remit, they are remitted to them; and whosoever sins you retain, they are retained.   JOHN 20:21–23

And, being assembled together with them, commanded them that they should not depart from Jerusalem, but wait for the promise of the Father, which, says He, you have heard of Me. For John truly baptized with water; but you shall be baptized with the Holy Ghost not many days from now.   ACTS 1:4–5

And suddenly there came a sound from heaven as of a rushing mighty wind, and it filled all the house where they were sitting.   ACTS 2:2

And it shall come to pass in the last days, says God, I will pour out of My Spirit upon all flesh: and your sons and your daughters shall prophesy, and your young men shall see visions, and your old men shall dream dreams: and on My servants and on My handmaidens I will pour out in those days of My Spirit; and they shall prophesy.   ACTS 2:17–18

And now, Lord, behold their threatenings: and grant to Your servants, that with all boldness they may speak Your word, by stretching forth Your hand to heal; and that signs and wonders may be done by the name of Your holy child Jesus.

ACTS 4:29–30

And when they had prayed, the place was shaken where they were assembled together; and they were all filled with the Holy Ghost, and they spoke the word of God with boldness. ACTS 4:31

And with great power gave the apostles witness of the resurrection of the Lord Jesus: and great grace was upon them all.

ACTS 4:33

And we are His witnesses of these things; and so is also the Holy Ghost, whom God has given to them that obey Him.

ACTS 5:32

You stiffnecked and uncircumcised in heart and ears, you do always resist the Holy Ghost: as your fathers did, so do you.

ACTS 7:51

And it came to pass, that, while Apollos was at Corinth, Paul having passed through the upper coasts came to Ephesus: and finding certain disciples, He said to them, Have you received the Holy Ghost since you believed? And they said to him, We have not so much as heard whether there be any Holy Ghost. And he said to them, To what then were you baptized? And they said, To John's baptism. Then said Paul, John verily baptized with the baptism of repentance, saying to the people, that they should believe on Him which should come after Him, that is, on Christ Jesus. When they heard this, they were baptized in the name of the Lord Jesus. And when Paul had laid his hands upon them, the Holy Ghost came on them; and they spoke with tongues, and prophesied. Acts 19:1–6

And not only so, but we glory in tribulations also: knowing that tribulation works patience; and patience, experience; and experience, hope: and hope makes not ashamed; because the love of God is shed abroad in our hearts by the Holy Ghost which is given to us. Romans 5:3–5

INSIGHTS ON FAITH FROM SMITH WIGGLESWORTH

The Holy Spirit has a royal plan, a heavenly plan. He came to unveil the King, to show the character of God, to unveil the precious blood of Jesus. Because I have the Holy Spirit within me, I see Jesus clothed for humanity. He was moved by the Spirit, led by the Spirit. We read of some who heard the Word of God but did not benefit from it because faith was lacking in them (Heb. 4:2). We must have a living faith in God's Word, a faith that is quickened by the Spirit.

~

The baptism of the Spirit has come for nothing less than to possess the whole of our lives. It sets up Jesus as King, and nothing can stand in His holy presence when He is made King. Everything will wither before Him.

~

The power of the Holy Spirit has to come to be enthroned in the human life so that it does not matter where we find ourselves. Christ is manifested in the place where devils are, the place where religious devils are, the place where false religion and unbelief are, the place where formal religion has taken the place of holiness and righteousness. You need to have holiness—the righteousness and Spirit of the Master—so that in every walk of life, everything that is not like our Lord Jesus will have to depart. That is what is needed today.

THE PERSON OF THE HOLY SPIRIT

There is therefore now no condemnation to them which are in Christ Jesus, who walk not after the flesh, but after the Spirit. For the law of the Spirit of life in Christ Jesus has made me free from the law of sin and death.   ROMANS 8:1–2

For you have not received the spirit of bondage again to fear; but you have received the Spirit of adoption, whereby we cry, Abba, Father.   ROMANS 8:15

Likewise the Spirit also helps our infirmities: for we know not what we should pray for as we ought: but the Spirit itself makes intercession for us with groanings which cannot be uttered. And He that searches the hearts knows what is the mind of the Spirit, because He makes intercession for the saints according to the will of God.   ROMANS 8:26–27

But as it is written, Eye has not seen, nor ear heard, neither have entered into the heart of man, the things which God has prepared for them that love Him. But God has revealed them to us by His Spirit: for the Spirit searches all things, yea, the deep things of God.   1 CORINTHIANS 2:9–10

Which things also we speak, not in the words which man's wisdom teaches, but which the Holy Ghost teaches; comparing spiritual things with spiritual. But the natural man receives not the things of the Spirit of God: for they are foolishness to him: neither can he know them, because they are spiritually discerned.

1 CORINTHIANS 2:13–14

Know you not that you are the temple of God, and that the Spirit of God dwells in you? If any man defile the temple of God, him shall God destroy; for the temple of God is holy, which temple you are.

1 CORINTHIANS 3:16–17

And such were some of you: but you are washed, but you are sanctified, but you are justified in the name of the Lord Jesus, and by the Spirit of our God.

1 CORINTHIANS 6:11

Now concerning spiritual gifts, brethren, I would not have you ignorant. You know that you were Gentiles, carried away to these dumb idols, even as you were led. Wherefore I give you to understand, that no man speaking by the Spirit of God calls Jesus accursed: and that no man can say that Jesus is the Lord, but by the Holy Ghost. Now there are diversities of gifts, but the same Spirit.

1 CORINTHIANS 12:1–4

But the manifestation of the Spirit is given to every man to profit withal. 1 CORINTHIANS 12:7

Forasmuch as you are manifestly declared to be the epistle of Christ ministered by us, written not with ink, but with the Spirit of the living God; not in tables of stone, but in fleshy tables of the heart. 2 CORINTHIANS 3:3

Not that we are sufficient of ourselves to think any thing as of ourselves; but our sufficiency is of God; who also has made us able ministers of the new testament; not of the letter, but of the Spirit: for the letter kills, but the Spirit gives life. 2 CORINTHIANS 3:5–6

Now the Lord is that Spirit: and where the Spirit of the Lord is, there is liberty. 2 CORINTHIANS 3:17

Now He that has wrought us for the selfsame thing is God, who also has given to us the earnest of the Spirit. 2 CORINTHIANS 5:5

INSIGHTS ON FAITH FROM SMITH WIGGLESWORTH

There are three things that ought to take place at the baptism of the Holy Spirit. It was necessary that the movement of the mighty rushing wind was made manifest in the Upper Room and that the disciples were clothed with tongues as of fire. (See Acts 2:1–4.) Also, it was necessary that they received not only the fire but also the rushing wind, the personality of the Spirit in the wind. The manifestation of the glory is in the wind, or breath, of God.

When we are baptized in the Holy Spirit, it is to crown Jesus King in our lives. Not only is the King to be within us, but also all the glories of His kingly manifestations are to be brought forth in us. Oh, for Him to work in us in this way, melting us, until a new order rises within us so that we are moved with His compassion. I see that we can come into the order of God where the vision becomes so much brighter and where the Lord is manifesting His glory with all His virtues and gifts; all His glory seems to fill the soul who is absolutely dead to himself and alive to God.

THE PERSON OF THE HOLY SPIRIT

That the blessing of Abraham might come on the Gentiles through Jesus Christ; that we might receive the promise of the Spirit through faith.　　　　　　　　　　　　　GALATIANS 3:14

And because you are sons, God has sent forth the Spirit of His Son into your hearts, crying, Abba, Father.　　　GALATIANS 4:6

In whom you also trusted, after that you heard the word of truth, the gospel of your salvation: in whom also after that you believed, you were sealed with that holy Spirit of promise, which is the earnest of our inheritance until the redemption of the purchased possession, to the praise of His glory.　　　EPHESIANS 1:13–14

That He would grant you, according to the riches of His glory, to be strengthened with might by His Spirit in the inner man.
　　　　　　　　　　　　　　　　　　　EPHESIANS 3:16

There is one body, and one Spirit, even as you are called in one hope of your calling.　　　　　　　　　　EPHESIANS 4:4

And grieve not the Holy Spirit of God, whereby you are sealed to the day of redemption.　　　　　　　　　EPHESIANS 4:30

And be not drunk with wine, wherein is excess; but be filled with the Spirit.　　　　　　　　　　　　　EPHESIANS 5:18

For we wrestle not against flesh and blood, but against principalities, against powers, against the rulers of the darkness of this world, against spiritual wickedness in high places.

EPHESIANS 6:12

And you became followers of us, and of the Lord, having received the word in much affliction, with joy of the Holy Ghost.

1 THESSALONIANS 1:6

Now the Spirit speaks expressly, that in the latter times some shall depart from the faith, giving heed to seducing spirits, and doctrines of devils.

1 TIMOTHY 4:1

Not by works of righteousness which we have done, but according to His mercy He saved us, by the washing of regeneration, and renewing of the Holy Ghost; which He shed on us abundantly through Jesus Christ our Savior.

TITUS 3:5–6

How much more shall the blood of Christ, who through the eternal Spirit offered Himself without spot to God, purge your conscience from dead works to serve the living God?

HEBREWS 9:14

If you be reproached for the name of Christ, happy are you; for the spirit of glory and of God rests upon you: on their part He is evil spoken of, but on your part He is glorified.

1 PETER 4:14

INSIGHTS ON FAITH FROM SMITH WIGGLESWORTH

The Spirit of God wants us to understand there is nothing that can interfere with our coming into perfect blessing except unbelief. Unbelief is a terrible hindrance. As soon as we are willing to allow the Holy Spirit to have His way, we will find that great things will happen all the time.

⌒

We are called to walk together with God through the Spirit. It is delightful to know that we can talk with God and hold communion with Him. Through this wonderful baptism in the Spirit that the Lord gives us, He enables us to talk to Him in a language that the Spirit has given, a language that no man understands but that He understands, a language of love. Oh, how wonderful it is to speak to Him in the Spirit, to let the Spirit lift and lift and lift us until He takes us into the very presence of God!

⌒

To be filled with the Holy Spirit is to be filled with the Executive of the Godhead, who brings to us all that the Father has and all that the Son desires, and we should be so in the Spirit that God can cause us to move with His authority and reign by His divine ability.

BEING SPIRIT-FILLED

But truly I am full of power by the Spirit of the LORD, and of judgment, and of might, to declare to Jacob his transgression, and to Israel his sin. MICAH 3:8

And it came to pass, that, when Elisabeth heard the salutation of Mary, the babe leaped in her womb; and Elisabeth was filled with the Holy Ghost. LUKE 1:41

God is a Spirit: and they that worship Him must worship Him in spirit and in truth. JOHN 4:24

Wherefore, brethren, look you out among you seven men of honest report, full of the Holy Ghost and wisdom, whom we may appoint over this business. ACTS 6:3

But you are not in the flesh, but in the Spirit, if so be that the Spirit of God dwell in you. Now if any man have not the Spirit of Christ, he is none of His. ROMANS 8:9

But all these works that one and the selfsame Spirit, dividing to every man severally as He will. 1 CORINTHIANS 12:11

For by one Spirit are we all baptized into one body, whether we be Jews or Gentiles, whether we be bond or free; and have been all made to drink into one Spirit.   1 CORINTHIANS 12:13

But we all, with open face beholding as in a glass the glory of the Lord, are changed into the same image from glory to glory, even as by the Spirit of the Lord.   2 CORINTHIANS 3:18

This I say then, Walk in the Spirit, and you shall not fulfill the lust of the flesh. For the flesh lusts against the Spirit, and the Spirit against the flesh: and these are contrary the one to the other: so that you cannot do the things that you would. But if you be led of the Spirit, you are not under the law.   GALATIANS 5:16–18

If we live in the Spirit, let us also walk in the Spirit.
        GALATIANS 5:25

Be filled with the Spirit; speaking to yourselves in psalms and hymns and spiritual songs, singing and making melody in your heart to the Lord; giving thanks always for all things to God and the Father in the name of our Lord Jesus Christ; submitting yourselves one to another in the fear of God.   EPHESIANS 5:18–21

Finally, my brethren, be strong in the Lord, and in the power of His might. Put on the whole armor of God, that you may be able to stand against the wiles of the devil. For we wrestle not against flesh and blood, but against principalities, against powers, against the rulers of the darkness of this world, against spiritual wickedness in high places. EPHESIANS 6:10–12

Praying always with all prayer and supplication in the Spirit, and watching thereto with all perseverance and supplication for all saints; and for me, that utterance may be given to me, that I may open my mouth boldly, to make known the mystery of the gospel. EPHESIANS 6:18–19

As you have therefore received Christ Jesus the Lord, so walk you in Him. COLOSSIANS 2:6

Quench not the Spirit. 1 THESSALONIANS 5:19

Seeing you have purified your souls in obeying the truth through the Spirit to unfeigned love of the brethren, see that you love one another with a pure heart fervently. 1 PETER 1:22

INSIGHTS ON FAITH FROM SMITH WIGGLESWORTH

Divine wisdom will never make you foolish. Divine wisdom will give you a sound mind; divine wisdom will give you a touch of divine nature. Divine life is full of divine appointment and equipping, and you cannot be filled with the power of God without a manifestation. It is my prayer today that we would understand that to be filled with the Holy Spirit is to be filled with manifestation, the glory of the Lord being in the midst of us, manifesting His divine power.

◡

Jesus spoke, and everything He said must come to pass. That is the great plan. When we are filled only with the Holy Spirit, and we won't allow the Word of God to be taken away by what we hear or by what we read, then comes the inspiration, then the life, then the activity, then the glory!

◡

When the Holy Spirit gets possession of a person, he is a new man entirely—his whole being becomes saturated with divine power. We become a habitation of Him who is all light, all revelation, all power, and all love. Yes, God the Holy Spirit is manifested within us in such a way that it is glorious.

WALKING WITH THE HOLY SPIRIT

You shall walk in all the ways which the LORD your God has commanded you, that you may live, and that it may be well with you, and that you may prolong your days in the land which you shall possess.   DEUTERONOMY 5:33

I was also upright before Him, and I kept myself from my iniquity.   PSALM 18:23

Order my steps in Your word: and let not any iniquity have dominion over me.   PSALM 119:133

My son, forget not my law; but let your heart keep my commandments: for length of days, and long life, and peace, shall they add to you. Let not mercy and truth forsake you: bind them about your neck; write them upon the table of your heart: so shall you find favor and good understanding in the sight of God and man.   PROVERBS 3:1–4

Trust in the LORD with all your heart; and lean not to your own understanding. In all your ways acknowledge Him, and He shall direct your paths.   PROVERBS 3:5–6

My son, keep my words, and lay up my commandments with you. Keep my commandments, and live; and my law as the apple of your eye. Bind them on your fingers, write them upon the table of your heart. PROVERBS 7:1–3

He has showed you, O man, what is good; and what does the LORD require of you, but to do justly, and to love mercy, and to walk humbly with your God? MICAH 6:8

You shall know them by their fruits. Do men gather grapes of thorns, or figs of thistles? MATTHEW 7:16

Heal the sick, cleanse the lepers, raise the dead, cast out devils: freely you have received, freely give. MATTHEW 10:8

He says to him the third time, Simon, son of Jonas, love you Me? Peter was grieved because He said to him the third time, Love you Me? And He said to him, Lord, You know all things; You know that I love You. Jesus says to him, Feed My sheep. JOHN 21:17

And we know that all things work together for good to them that love God, to them who are the called according to His purpose. ROMANS 8:28

For we are His workmanship, created in Christ Jesus to good works, which God has before ordained that we should walk in them.   EPHESIANS 2:10

For you were sometimes darkness, but now are you light in the Lord: walk as children of light: (For the fruit of the Spirit is in all goodness and righteousness and truth).   EPHESIANS 5:8–9

Examine yourselves, whether you be in the faith; prove your own selves. Know you not your own selves, how that Jesus Christ is in you, except you be reprobates?   2 CORINTHIANS 13:5

Wherefore the rather, brethren, give diligence to make your calling and election sure: for if you do these things, you shall never fall.   2 PETER 1:10

Whosoever is born of God does not commit sin; for His seed remains in him: and he cannot sin, because he is born of God.   1 JOHN 3:9

INSIGHTS ON FAITH FROM SMITH WIGGLESWORTH

When the Holy Spirit comes, He will reveal things to you. Has He revealed them yet? He is going to do it. Just expect Him to do so. The best thing for you is to expect Him to do it now.

⌒

God the Holy Spirit wants to bring us to a great revelation of life. He wants us to be filled with all the fullness of God. One of the most beautiful pictures we have in the Scriptures is of the Trinity. The Trinity was made manifest right on the banks of the Jordan River when Jesus was baptized. I want you to see how God unfolded heaven and how heaven and earth became the habitation of the Trinity. The voice of God came from the heavens as He looked at His well-beloved Son coming out of the waters, and there the Spirit was manifested in the shape of a dove. The dove is the only bird without gall; it is a creature so timid that at the least thing it moves and is afraid. No person can be baptized with the Holy Spirit and have bitterness, that is, gall.

"AFTER THE HOLY SPIRIT COMES UPON YOU, YOU WILL HAVE POWER. GOD WILL MIGHTILY MOVE WITHIN YOUR LIFE; THE POWER OF THE HOLY SPIRIT WILL OVERSHADOW YOU, INWARDLY MOVING YOU UNTIL YOU KNOW THERE IS A DIVINE PLAN DIFFERENT FROM ANYTHING THAT YOU HAVE HAD IN YOUR LIFE BEFORE."

—SMITH WIGGLESWORTH

2

ENCOUNTERING THE HOLY SPIRIT

THE ANOINTING OF THE HOLY SPIRIT

And I will raise Me up a faithful priest, that shall do according to that which is in My heart and in My mind: and I will build him a sure house; and he shall walk before My anointed for ever.

1 SAMUEL 2:35

Now know I that the LORD saves His anointed; He will hear him from His holy heaven with the saving strength of His right hand.

PSALM 20:6

You love righteousness, and hate wickedness: therefore God, Your God, has anointed You with the oil of gladness above Your fellows.

PSALM 45:7

Where shall I go from Your spirit? or where shall I flee from Your presence?

PSALM 139:7

And it shall come to pass in that day, that his burden shall be taken away from off your shoulder, and his yoke from off your neck, and the yoke shall be destroyed because of the anointing.

ISAIAH 10:27

And the spirit of the LORD shall rest upon Him, the spirit of wisdom and understanding, the spirit of counsel and might, the spirit of knowledge and of the fear of the LORD.   ISAIAH 11:2

The Spirit of the LORD God is upon me; because the LORD has anointed me to preach good tidings to the meek; He has sent me to bind up the brokenhearted, to proclaim liberty to the captives, and the opening of the prison to them that are bound; to proclaim the acceptable year of the LORD, and the day of vengeance of our God; to comfort all that mourn.   ISAIAH 61:1–2

To appoint to them that mourn in Zion, to give to them beauty for ashes, the oil of joy for mourning, the garment of praise for the spirit of heaviness; that they might be called trees of righteousness, the planting of the LORD, that He might be glorified.

ISAIAH 61:3

Then he answered and spoke to me, saying, This is the word of the LORD to Zerubbabel, saying, Not by might, nor by power, but by My spirit, says the LORD of hosts.   ZECHARIAH 4:6

And Jesus, when he was baptized, went up straightway out of the water: and, lo, the heavens were opened to Him, and he saw the Spirit of God descending like a dove, and lighting upon Him.

MATTHEW 3:16

Take My yoke upon you, and learn of Me; for I am meek and lowly in heart: and you shall find rest to your souls.

MATTHEW 11:29

But if I cast out devils by the Spirit of God, then the kingdom of God is come to you.

MATTHEW 12:28

Go you therefore, and teach all nations, baptizing them in the name of the Father, and of the Son, and of the Holy Ghost.

MATTHEW 28:19

The Spirit of the Lord is upon me, because He has anointed me to preach the gospel to the poor; He has sent me to heal the broken-hearted, to preach deliverance to the captives, and recovering of sight to the blind, to set at liberty them that are bruised, to preach the acceptable year of the Lord.

LUKE 4:18–19

INSIGHTS ON FAITH FROM SMITH WIGGLESWORTH

The Holy Spirit is not a touch or a breath. He is the Almighty God. He is a person. He is the Holy One dwelling in the temple *"not made with hands"* (2 Cor. 5:1). Beloved, He touches, and it is done. He is the same God over all who is rich unto all who call upon Him (Rom. 10:12).

~

God has a plan for us in this life of the Spirit, this abundant life. Jesus came so that we might have life (John 10:10). Satan comes to steal and kill and destroy (v. 10), but God has abundance for us—full measure, pressed down, shaken together, overflowing, abundant measure (Luke 6:38). This abundance is God filling us with His own personality and presence, making us salt and light and giving us a revelation of Himself.

~

When we are clothed with the Spirit, our human depravity is covered and everything that is contrary to the mind of God is destroyed. God must have people for Himself who are being clothed with a heavenly habitation, perfectly prepared by the Holy Spirit for the Day of the Lord. *"For in this we groan, earnestly desiring to be clothed with our habitation which is from heaven"* (1 Cor. 5:2).

THE ANOINTING OF THE HOLY SPIRIT

If you then, being evil, know how to give good gifts to your children: how much more shall your heavenly Father give the Holy Spirit to them that ask Him?　　　　　　LUKE 11:13

And, behold, I send the promise of My Father upon you: but tarry you in the city of Jerusalem, until you be endued with power from on high.　　　　　　LUKE 24:49

And John bore record, saying, I saw the Spirit descending from heaven like a dove, and it abode upon Him.　　　　　　JOHN 1:32

It is the spirit that quickens; the flesh profits nothing: the words that I speak to you, they are spirit, and they are life.　　JOHN 6:63

Believe you not that I am in the Father, and the Father in Me? the words that I speak to you I speak not of Myself: but the Father that dwells in Me, He does the works.　　　　　　JOHN 14:10

Even the Spirit of truth; whom the world cannot receive, because it sees Him not, neither knows Him: but you know Him; for He dwells with you, and shall be in you.　　　　　　JOHN 14:17

But the Comforter, which is the Holy Ghost, whom the Father will send in My name, He shall teach you all things, and bring all things to your remembrance, whatsoever I have said to you.
JOHN 14:26

However when He, the Spirit of truth, is come, He will guide you into all truth: for He shall not speak of Himself; but whatsoever He shall hear, that shall He speak: and He will show you things to come. John 16:13

But you shall receive power, after that the Holy Ghost is come upon you: and you shall be witnesses to Me both in Jerusalem, and in all Judaea, and in Samaria, and to the uttermost part of the earth. Acts 1:8

And they were all filled with the Holy Ghost, and began to speak with other tongues, as the Spirit gave them utterance. Acts 2:4

Therefore being by the right hand of God exalted, and having received of the Father the promise of the Holy Ghost, He has shed forth this, which you now see and hear. Acts 2:33

Then Peter said to them, Repent, and be baptized every one of you in the name of Jesus Christ for the remission of sins, and you shall receive the gift of the Holy Ghost. Acts 2:38

But he, being full of the Holy Ghost, looked up steadfastly into heaven, and saw the glory of God, and Jesus standing on the right hand of God. Acts 7:55

INSIGHTS ON FAITH FROM SMITH WIGGLESWORTH

It is indeed the name of Jesus that brings power over evil spirits, only they did not understand it. Oh, that God would help us to understand the name of Jesus! There is something in that name that attracts the whole world. It is the name, oh, it is still the name, but you must understand that there is the ministry of the name. It is the Holy Spirit who is behind the ministry. The power is in the knowledge of Him; it is in the ministry of the knowledge of Him, and I can understand that it is only that.

The Holy Spirit has come with one definite purpose, and that is to reveal to us the Father and the Son in all their different branches of helpfulness to humanity. The Spirit has come to display almighty power so that the weak may be made strong, and to bring to sickness such a manifestation of the blood of Christ, of the Atonement on Calvary, that the evil power of disease is conquered and forced to leave.

In this baptism of the Holy Spirit, there is a holy boldness—not superstition, but a boldness that stands unflinchingly and truly on what the Word of God says. To have holy boldness is to live in the Holy Spirit, to get to know the principles that are worked out by Him.

THE ANOINTING OF THE HOLY SPIRIT

And it cam to pass, when they were gone over, that Elijah said to Elisha, Ask what I shall do for you, before I be taken away from you. and Elisha said, I pray you, let a double portion of your spirit be upon me.   2 KINGS 2:9

Now when the apostles which were at Jerusalem heard that Samaria had received the word of God, they sent to them Peter and John: who, when they were come down, prayed for them, that they might receive the Holy Ghost: (for as yet He was fallen upon none of them: only they were baptized in the name of the Lord Jesus.) Then laid they their hands on them, and they received the Holy Ghost.   ACTS 8:14–17

And when they were come up out of the water, the Spirit of the Lord caught away Philip, that the eunuch saw him no more: and he went on his way rejoicing.   ACTS 8:39

How God anointed Jesus of Nazareth with the Holy Ghost and with power: who went about doing good, and healing all that were oppressed of the devil; for God was with Him.   ACTS 10:38

Then remembered I the word of the Lord, how that He said, John indeed baptized with water; but you shall be baptized with the Holy Ghost. ACTS 11:16

There is therefore now no condemnation to them which are in Christ Jesus, who walk not after the flesh, but after the Spirit. For the law of the Spirit of life in Christ Jesus have made me free from the law of sin and death. For what the law could not do, in that it was weak through the flesh, God sending His own Son in the likeness of sinful flesh, and for sin, condemned sin in the flesh: that the righteousness of the law might be fulfilled in us, who walk not after the flesh, but after the Spirit. For they that are after the flesh do mind the things of the flesh; but they that are after the Spirit the things of the Spirit. ROMANS 8:1–5

But you are not in the flesh, but in the Spirit, if so be that the Spirit of God dwell in you. Now if any man have not the Spirit of Christ, he is none of His. ROMANS 8:9

But if the Spirit of him that raised up Jesus from the dead dwell in you, He that raised up Christ from the dead shall also quicken your mortal bodies by His Spirit that dwells in you.

ROMANS 8:11

For as many as are led by the Spirit of God, they are the sons of God.   ROMANS 8:14

The Spirit itself bears witness with our spirit, that we are the children of God.   ROMANS 8:16

Now the God of hope fill you with all joy and peace in believing, that you may abound in hope, through the power of the Holy Ghost.   ROMANS 15:13

For Christ sent me not to baptize, but to preach the gospel: not with wisdom of words, lest the cross of Christ should be made of none effect.   1 CORINTHIANS 1:17

And my speech and my preaching was not with enticing words of man's wisdom, but in demonstration of the Spirit and of power: that your faith should not stand in the wisdom of men, but in the power of God.   1 CORINTHIANS 2:4–5

Know you not that you are the temple of God, and that the Spirit of God dwells in you?   1 CORINTHIANS 3:16

INSIGHTS ON FAITH FROM SMITH WIGGLESWORTH

Why should we tarry for the Holy Ghost? Why should we wrestle and pray for living faith to be made ready? In John 16:7–8, we find the reason: "*It is expedient for you that I go away: for if I go not away, the Comforter will not come unto you; but if I depart, I will send him unto you. And when he is come, he will reprove the world of sin, and of righteousness, and of judgment.*"

⤳

That is why the Holy Ghost is to come into your body. First of all, when your sin is gone, you can see clearly to speak to others. But Jesus does not want you to pick the mote out of someone else's eye while a beam remains in your own eye. (See Matthew 7:1–5.) When your own sins are gone, then the Holy Ghost is to convince the world of sin, of righteousness, and of judgment.

⤳

Only when a person is filled with the Holy Ghost can he bind the power of Satan. Satan has a right, he thinks, and will have a short time to exhibit it as the prince of the world, but he can't be prince as long as there is one person filled with the Holy Ghost. That is the reason why the church will go before tribulation.

THE ANOINTING OF THE HOLY SPIRIT

What? know you not that your body is the temple of the Holy Ghost which is in you, which you have of God, and you are not your own?   1 CORINTHIANS 6:19

Wherefore I give you to understand, that no man speaking by the Spirit of God calls Jesus accursed: and that no man can say that Jesus is the Lord, but by the Holy Ghost.
                                                        1 CORINTHIANS 12:3

For to one is given by the Spirit the word of wisdom; to another the word of knowledge by the same Spirit; to another faith by the same Spirit; to another the gifts of healing by the same Spirit; to another the working of miracles; to another prophecy; to another discerning of spirits; to another divers kinds of tongues; to another the interpretation of tongues.   1 CORINTHIANS 12:8–10

Now He which establishes us with you in Christ, and has anointed us, is God.   2 CORINTHIANS 1:21

This I say then, Walk in the Spirit, and you shall not fulfill the lust of the flesh.   GALATIANS 5:16

And take the helmet of salvation, and the sword of the Spirit, which is the word of God.   EPHESIANS 6:17

For the Lord Himself shall descend from heaven with a shout, with the voice of the archangel, and with the trump of God: and the dead in Christ shall rise first: then we which are alive and remain shall be caught up together with them in the clouds, to meet the Lord in the air: and so shall we ever be with the Lord. Wherefore comfort one another with these words.
                    1 THESSALONIANS 4:16–18

Elect according to the foreknowledge of God the Father, through sanctification of the Spirit, to obedience and sprinkling of the blood of Jesus Christ: Grace to you, and peace, be multiplied.
                    1 PETER 1:2

For the prophecy came not in old time by the will of man: but holy men of God spoke as they were moved by the Holy Ghost.
                    2 PETER 1:21

But if we walk in the light, as He is in the light, we have fellowship one with another, and the blood of Jesus Christ His Son cleanses us from all sin.   1 JOHN 1:7

But you have an unction from the Holy One, and you know all things. I have not written to you because you know not the truth, but because you know it, and that no lie is of the truth. Who is a liar but he that denies that Jesus is the Christ? He is antichrist, that denies the Father and the Son.   1 JOHN 2:20–22

But the anointing which you have received of Him abides in you, and you need not that any man teach you: but as the same anointing teaches you of all things, and is truth, and is no lie, and even as it has taught you, you shall abide in him.   1 JOHN 2:27

Beloved, believe not every spirit, but try the spirits whether they are of God: because many false prophets are gone out into the world.   1 JOHN 4:1

We are of God: he that knows God hears us; he that is not of God hears not us. Hereby know we the spirit of truth, and the spirit of error.   1 JOHN 4:6

INSIGHTS ON FAITH FROM SMITH WIGGLESWORTH

The gift of the Holy Ghost, when He has breathed in you, will make you alive so that it is wonderful; it seems almost then as though you had never been born. The jealousy God has over us, the interest He has in us, the purpose He has for us, the grandeur of His glory, are so marvelous that God has called us into this place to receive gifts.

When God begins dealing with you on the baptism, He begins on this line: He starts with the things which are the most difficult. He starts with your human nature. He starts with your fear. He gets the fear away, gets the human nature out of place; and just as you dissolve, just as the power of the Spirit brings a dissolving to your human nature, in the same act, the Holy Ghost flows into the place where you are being dissolved, and you are quickened just where you come into death. And as you die—naturally, humanly, carnally, selfishly—of every evil thing, the new life, the Holy Ghost floods the whole case till it becomes a transformed case.

CLOTHED WITH THE SPIRIT

Then touched He their eyes, saying, According to your faith be it to you.   Matthew 9:29

As soon as Jesus heard the word that was spoken, He said to the ruler of the synagogue, Be not afraid, only believe.   Mark 5:36

And Jesus answering said to them, Have faith in God.   Mark 11:22

Give, and it shall be given to you; good measure, pressed down, and shaken together, and running over, shall men give into your bosom. For with the same measure that you mete withal it shall be measured to you again.   Luke 6:38

But He turned, and rebuked them, and said, You know not what manner of spirit you are of.   Luke 9:55

God is a Spirit: and they that worship Him must worship Him in spirit and in truth.   John 4:24

The thief comes not, but for to steal, and to kill, and to destroy: I am come that they might have life, and that they might have it more abundantly.   John 10:10

But the Comforter, which is the Holy Ghost, whom the Father will send in My name, He shall teach you all things, and bring all things to your remembrance, whatsoever I have said to you.

JOHN 14:26

But you shall receive power, after that the Holy Ghost is come upon you: and you shall be witnesses to Me both in Jerusalem, and in all Judaea, and in Samaria, and to the uttermost part of the earth.

ACTS 1:8

Then Peter said to them, Repent, and be baptized every one of you in the name of Jesus Christ for the remission of sins, and you shall receive the gift of the Holy Ghost.

ACTS 2:38

Because the carnal mind is enmity against God: for it is not subject to the law of God, neither indeed can be.

ROMANS 8:7

That if you shall confess with your mouth the Lord Jesus, and shall believe in your heart that God has raised Him from the dead, you shall be saved.

ROMANS 10:9

Moreover, brethren, I would not that you should be ignorant, how that all our fathers were under the cloud, and all passed through the sea.

1 CORINTHIANS 10:1

For we know that if our earthly house of this tabernacle were dissolved, we have a building of God, an house not made with hands, eternal in the heavens.... For we that are in this tabernacle do groan, being burdened: not for that we would be unclothed, but clothed upon, that mortality might be swallowed up of life. Now He that has wrought us for the selfsame thing is God, who also has given to us the earnest of the Spirit.   2 CORINTHIANS 5:1, 4–5

This I say then, Walk in the Spirit, and you shall not fulfill the lust of the flesh.   GALATIANS 5:16

That you put off concerning the former conversation the old man, which is corrupt according to the deceitful lusts; and be renewed in the spirit of your mind; and that you put on the new man, which after God is created in righteousness and true holiness.

EPHESIANS 4:22–24

INSIGHTS ON FAITH FROM SMITH WIGGLESWORTH

Most of us have seen water baptism in action so often that we know what it means. But I want you to see that God's very great desire is for you to be covered with the baptism of the Holy Spirit. He wants you to be so immersed and covered and flooded with the light and revelation of the Holy Spirit, the third person of the Trinity, that your whole body will be filled, and not only filled but also covered over until you walk in the presence of the power of God.

❧

The baptism of the Holy Spirit is the essential, mighty touch of revelation of the wonders, for God the Holy Spirit has no limitations along these lines. But when the soul is ready to enter into His life, there is a breaking up of fallow ground and a moving of the mists away, bringing us into the perfect day of the light of God.

❧

You can never be the same again after you have received this wonderful baptism in the Holy Spirit. It is important that we should be full of wisdom and faith day by day and full of the Holy Spirit, acting by the power of the Holy Spirit. God has set us here in the last days, these days of apostasy, and wants us to be burning and shining lights in the midst of an indecent generation.

CLOTHED WITH THE SPIRIT

That you put off concerning the former conversation the old man, which is corrupt according to the deceitful lusts; and be renewed in the spirit of your mind; and that you put on the new man, which after God is created in righteousness and true holiness.

EPHESIANS 4:22–24

For you are dead, and your life is hid with Christ in God.

COLOSSIANS 3:3

Who has saved us, and called us with a holy calling, not according to our works, but according to His own purpose and grace, which was given us in Christ Jesus before the world began, but is now made manifest by the appearing of our Savior Jesus Christ, who has abolished death, and has brought life and immortality to light through the gospel.

2 TIMOTHY 1:9–10

For to us was the gospel preached, as well as to them: but the word preached did not profit them, not being mixed with faith in them that heard it.

HEBREWS 4:2

Beloved, believe not every spirit, but try the spirits whether they are of God: because many false prophets are gone out into the world.

1 JOHN 4:1

BIBLICAL EVIDENCE OF THE HOLY SPIRIT BAPTISM

A new heart also will I give you, and a new Spirit will I put within you: and I will take away the stony heart out of your flesh, and I will give you a heart of flesh. And I will put My Spirit within you, and cause you to walk in My statutes, and you shall keep My judgments, and do them. EZEKIEL 36:26–27

And it shall come to pass afterward, that I will pour out My Spirit upon all flesh; and your sons and your daughters shall prophesy, your old men shall dream dreams, your young men shall see visions: and also upon the servants and upon the handmaids in those days will I pour out My Spirit. JOEL 2:28–29

I indeed baptize you with water to repentance: but He that comes after me is mightier than I, whose shoes I am not worthy to bear: He shall baptize you with the Holy Ghost, and with fire.

MATTHEW 3:11

I indeed have baptized you with water: but He shall baptize you with the Holy Ghost. MARK 1:8

And He arose, and rebuked the wind, and said to the sea, Peace, be still. And the wind ceased, and there was a great calm.

MARK 4:39

He that believes and is baptized shall be saved; but he that believes not shall be damned.   MARK 16:16

And the angel answered and said to her, The Holy Ghost shall come upon you, and the power of the Highest shall overshadow you: therefore also that holy thing which shall be born of you shall be called the Son of God.   LUKE 1:35

Jesus answered, Verily, verily, I say to you, Except a man be born of water and of the Spirit, he cannot enter into the kingdom of God.   JOHN 3:5

(But this spoke He of the Spirit, which they that believe on Him should receive: for the Holy Ghost was not yet given; because that Jesus was not yet glorified.)   JOHN 7:39

And I will pray the Father, and He shall give you another Comforter, that He may abide with you for ever.

JOHN 14:16

INSIGHTS ON FAITH FROM SMITH WIGGLESWORTH

God wants to flow through you with measureless power of divine utterance and grace until your whole body is a flame of fire. God intends each soul in Pentecost to be a live wire—not a monument, but a movement. So many people have been baptized with the Holy Spirit; there was a movement, but they have become monuments, and you cannot move them. God, wake us out of sleep lest we should become indifferent to the glorious truth and the breath of the almighty power of God.

God wants you to be so balanced in spiritual anointing that you will always be able to do what pleases Him, and not what will please other people or yourself. The ideal must be that it will all be to edification, and everything must go on to this end to please the Lord.

BIBLICAL EVIDENCE OF THE HOLY SPIRIT BAPTISM

But when the Comforter is come, whom I will send to you from the Father, even the Spirit of truth, which proceeds from the Father, He shall testify of Me. JOHN 15:26

And when the day of Pentecost was fully come, they were all with one accord in one place. And suddenly there came a sound from heaven as of a rushing mighty wind, and it filled all the house where they were sitting. And there appeared to them cloven tongues like as of fire, and it sat upon each of them. And they were all filled with the Holy Ghost, and began to speak with other tongues, as the Spirit gave them utterance. ACTS 2:1–4

Then they that gladly received his word were baptized: and the same day there were added to them about three thousand souls. ACTS 2:41

Then Peter, filled with the Holy Ghost, said to them, You rulers of the people, and elders of Israel. ACTS 4:8

Then laid they their hands on them, and they received the Holy Ghost. ACTS 8:17

And they of the circumcision which believed were astonished, as many as came with Peter, because that on the Gentiles also was poured out the gift of the Holy Ghost. For they heard them speak with tongues, and magnify God.   ACTS 10: 45–46

And God, which knows the hearts, bore them witness, giving them the Holy Ghost, even as He did to us.   ACTS 15:8

And it came to pass, that, while Apollos was at Corinth, Paul having passed through the upper coasts came to Ephesus: and finding certain disciples, he said to them, Have you received the Holy Ghost since you believed? And they said to him, We have not so much as heard whether there be any Holy Ghost.

ACTS 19:1–2

And when Paul had laid his hands upon them, the Holy Ghost came on them; and they spoke with tongues, and prophesied.

ACTS 19:6

For by one Spirit are we all baptized into one body, whether we be Jews or Gentiles, whether we be bond or free; and have been all made to drink into one Spirit.   1 CORINTHIANS 12:13

He that speaks in an unknown tongue edifies himself; but he that prophesies edifies the church.   1 CORINTHIANS 14:4

In whom you also trusted, after that you heard the word of truth, the gospel of your salvation: in whom also after that you believed, you were sealed with that holy Spirit of promise.

EPHESIANS 1:13

And grieve not the Holy Spirit of God, whereby you are sealed to the day of redemption.   EPHESIANS 4:30

The like figure whereto even baptism does also now save us (not the putting away of the filth of the flesh, but the answer of a good conscience toward God,) by the resurrection of Jesus Christ.

1 PETER 3:21

"HALT! THINK! WHAT IS THE ATTITUDE OF YOUR LIFE? ARE YOU THIRSTY? ARE YOU LONGING? ARE YOU WILLING TO PAY THE PRICE? ARE YOU WILLING TO FORFEIT IN ORDER TO HAVE? ARE YOU WILLING TO ALLOW YOURSELF TO DIE THAT HE MAY LIVE? ARE YOU WILLING FOR HIM TO HAVE RIGHT-OF-WAY OF YOUR HEART, YOUR CONSCIENCE, AND ALL THAT YOU ARE? ARE YOU READY TO HAVE GOD'S DELUGE OF BLESSING POUR INTO YOUR SOUL?

—SMITH WIGGLESWORTH

3

THE FRUITS OF THE SPIRIT

LOVE

You shall not avenge, nor bear any grudge against the children of your people, but you shall love your neighbor as yourself: I am the Lord. LEVITICUS 19:18

But I say to you, Love your enemies, bless them that curse you, do good to them that hate you, and pray for them which despitefully use you, and persecute you; that you may be the children of your Father which is in heaven: for He makes His sun to rise on the evil and on the good, and sends rain on the just and on the unjust. For if you love them which love you, what reward have you? do not even the publicans the same? And if you salute your brethren only, what do you more than others? do not even the publicans so? Be you therefore perfect, even as your Father which is in heaven is perfect. MATTHEW 5:44–48

Jesus said to him, You shall love the Lord your God with all your heart, and with all your soul, and with all your mind.

MATTHEW 22:37

A new commandment I give to you, that you love one another; as I have loved you, that you also love one another. By this shall all men know that you are My disciples, if you have love one to another.

JOHN 13:34–35

As the Father has loved Me, so have I loved you: continue you in My love. If you keep My commandments, you shall abide in My love; even as I have kept my Father's commandments, and abide in His love. These things have I spoken to you, that My joy might remain in you, and that your joy might be full. This is My commandment, That you love one another, as I have loved you. Greater love has no man than this, that a man lay down his life for his friends.

JOHN 15:9–13

Owe no man any thing, but to love one another: for he that loves another has fulfilled the law.

ROMANS 13:8

Love works no ill to his neighbor: therefore love is the fulfilling of the law.

ROMANS 13:10

And now abides faith, hope, charity, these three; but the greatest of these is charity.   1 CORINTHIANS 13:13

Let all your things be done with charity. 1 CORINTHIANS 16:14

And above all these things put on charity, which is the bond of perfectness. And let the peace of God rule in your hearts, to the which also you are called in one body; and be you thankful.
                                          COLOSSIANS 3:14–15

Beloved, let us love one another: for love is of God; and every one that loves is born of God, and knows God. He that loves not knows not God; for God is love.   1 JOHN 4:7–8

And we have known and believed the love that God has to us. God is love; and he that dwells in love dwells in God, and God in him.... There is no fear in love; but perfect love casts out fear: because fear has torment. He that fears is not made perfect in love.   1 JOHN 4:16, 18

We love Him, because He first loved us.   1 JOHN 4:19

INSIGHTS ON FAITH FROM SMITH WIGGLESWORTH

God wants to show you that there is a place where we can live in the Spirit and not be subject to the flesh. We can live in the Spirit until sin has no dominion over us. We reign in life and see the covering of God over us in the Spirit. Sin reigned unto death, but Christ reigned over sin and death, and so we reign with Him in life.

⌒

The Holy Spirit breathes through us, enabling us to say, "You are my Father; You are my Father." Because you have been adopted, *"God has sent forth the Spirit of His Son into your hearts, crying out, 'Abba, Father!'"* (Gal. 4:6). Oh, it is wonderful. May God the Holy Spirit grant to us that richness of His pleasure, that unfolding of His will, that consciousness of His smile upon us. There is *"no condemnation"* (Rom. 8:1). We find that *"the law of the Spirit of life"* makes us *"free from the law of sin and death"* (v. 2). Glory!

⌒

Through the blood of Christ's atonement, we may have riches and riches. We need the warming atmosphere of the Spirit's power to bring us closer and closer until nothing but God can satisfy, and then we may have some idea of what God has left over after we have taken all that we can.

JOY

Then he said to them, Go your way, eat the fat, and drink the sweet, and send portions to them for whom nothing is prepared: for this day is holy to our LORD: neither be you sorry; for the joy of the LORD is your strength.   NEHEMIAH 8:10

For His anger endures but a moment; in His favor is life: weeping may endure for a night, but joy comes in the morning.
PSALM 30:5

My lips shall greatly rejoice when I sing to You; and my soul, which You have redeemed.   PSALM 71:23

Light is sown for the righteous, and gladness for the upright in heart. Rejoice in the LORD, you righteous; and give thanks at the remembrance of His holiness.   PSALM 97:11–12

He that goes forth and weeps, bearing precious seed, shall doubtless come again with rejoicing, bringing his sheaves with him.
PSALM 126:6

A merry heart does good like a medicine: but a broken spirit dries the bones.   PROVERBS 17:22

Then I commended mirth, because a man has no better thing under the sun, than to eat, and to drink, and to be merry: for that shall abide with him of his labor the days of his life, which God gives him under the sun.   ECCLESIASTES 8:15

For you shall go out with joy, and be led forth with peace: the mountains and the hills shall break forth before you into singing, and all the trees of the field shall clap their hands.

ISAIAH 55:12

I will greatly rejoice in the LORD, my soul shall be joyful in my God; for He has clothed me with the garments of salvation, He has covered me with the robe of righteousness, as a bridegroom decks himself with ornaments, and as a bride adorns herself with her jewels.   ISAIAH 61:10

Likewise, I say to you, there is joy in the presence of the angels of God over one sinner that repents.   LUKE 15:10

These things have I spoken to you, that My joy might remain in you, and that your joy might be full.   JOHN 15:11

And you now therefore have sorrow: but I will see you again, and your heart shall rejoice, and your joy no man take from you.

JOHN 16:22

Until now have you asked nothing in My name: ask, and you shall receive, that your joy may be full.   JOHN 16:24

For the kingdom of God is not meat and drink; but righteousness, and peace, and joy in the Holy Ghost.   ROMANS 14:17

Always in every prayer of mine for you all making request with joy.   PHILIPPIANS 1:4

Rejoice in the Lord always: and again I say, Rejoice.

PHILIPPIANS 4:4

My brethren, count it all joy when you fall into divers temptations; knowing this, that the trying of your faith works patience. But let patience have her perfect work, that you may be perfect and entire, wanting nothing.   JAMES 1:2–4

INSIGHTS ON FAITH FROM SMITH WIGGLESWORTH

Oh, the joy of being filled with the Holy Spirit, with divine purpose! Oh, the satisfaction of being active "*in season and out of season*" (2 Tim. 4:2) with the sense of divine approval. As the apostles were in their day, so we are to be in our day: "*filled with all the fullness of God*" (Eph. 3:19).

~

Beloved, the Holy Spirit is the Comforter. The Holy Spirit did not come to speak of Himself, but He came to unveil Him who said, "*Take My yoke upon you and learn from Me, for I am gentle and lowly in heart, and you will find rest for your souls*" (Matt. 11:29). The Holy Spirit came to thrill you with resurrection power, and He came so that you would be anointed "with fresh oil that overflows in the splendor of His almightiness.

~

He who comes to God is already in the place where the Holy Spirit takes the prayers and swings them out according to the mind of the Spirit. For who has known the mind of Christ, or who is able to make intercession, except the mind of the Spirit of the living God? He makes intercession. Where is He? He is in us.

PEACE

For you shall be in league with the stones of the field: and the beasts of the field shall be at peace with you. JOB 5:23

Deceit is in the heart of them that imagine evil: but to the counsellors of peace is joy. PROVERBS 12:20

When a man's ways please the LORD, He makes even his enemies to be at peace with him. PROVERBS 16:7

You will keep him in perfect peace, whose mind is stayed on You: because he trusts in You. ISAIAH 26:3

Fear you not; for I am with you: be not dismayed; for I am Your God: I will strengthen you; yea, I will help you; yea, I will uphold you with the right hand of My righteousness. ISAIAH 41:10

Behold, I will bring it health and cure, and I will cure them, and will reveal to them the abundance of peace and truth. JEREMIAH 33:6

The glory of this latter house shall be greater than of the former, says the LORD of hosts: and in this place will I give peace, says the LORD of hosts. HAGGAI 2:9

Take therefore no thought for the morrow: for the morrow shall take thought for the things of itself. Sufficient to the day is the evil thereof. MATTHEW 6:34

These things I have spoken to you, that in Me you might have peace. In the world you shall have tribulation: but be of good cheer; I have overcome the world. JOHN 16:33

Be careful for nothing; but in every thing by prayer and supplication with thanksgiving let your requests be made known to God. And the peace of God, which passes all understanding, shall keep your hearts and minds through Christ Jesus.

PHILIPPIANS 4:6–7

And the very God of peace sanctify you wholly; and I pray God your whole spirit and soul and body be preserved blameless to the coming of our Lord Jesus Christ. 1 THESSALONIANS 5:23

Now the Lord of peace himself give you peace always by all means. The Lord be with you all. 2 THESSALONIANS 3:16

Follow peace with all men, and holiness, without which no man shall see the Lord. HEBREWS 12:14

Let him eschew evil, and do good; let him seek peace, and ensue it. 1 PETER 3:11

Casting all your care upon him; for He cares for you.

1 PETER 5:7

INSIGHTS ON FAITH FROM SMITH WIGGLESWORTH

May God the Holy Spirit bring us into that blessed place where we may live, walk, pray, and sing in the Spirit, and pray and sing with the understanding, also. Faith will do it.

❧

Oh, tell me if you can, is there anything to compare to what Jesus said: *"When the Holy Spirit comes, 'He will teach you all things, and bring to your remembrance all things'"* (John 14:26)? Surely this is a Comforter. Surely He is the Comforter who can bring to our memories and minds all the things that Jesus said.

❧

Jesus was sent from God to meet the world's needs. Jesus lived to minister life by the words He spoke. He said to Philip, *"He who has seen Me has seen the Father…. The words that I speak to you I do not speak on my own authority; but the Father who dwells in Me"* (John 14:9–10). I am persuaded that if we are filled with His words of life and the Holy Spirit, and Christ is made manifest in our mortal flesh, then the Holy Spirit can really move us with His life and His words until as He was, so are we in the world.

PATIENCE

Rest in the LORD, and wait patiently for Him: fret not yourself because of him who prospers in his way, because of the man who brings wicked devices to pass. Cease from anger, and forsake wrath: fret not yourself in any wise to do evil. For evildoers shall be cut off: but those that wait upon the LORD, they shall inherit the earth.   PSALM 37:7–9

I wait for the LORD, my soul does wait, and in His word do I hope.   PSALM 130:5

Better is the end of a thing than the beginning thereof: and the patient in spirit is better than the proud in spirit. Be not hasty in your spirit to be angry: for anger rests in the bosom of fools.
                                                       ECCLESIASTES 7:8–9

Even the youths shall faint and be weary, and the young men shall utterly fall: But they that wait upon the LORD shall renew their strength; they shall mount up with wings as eagles; they shall run, and not be weary; and they shall walk, and not faint.
                                                       ISAIAH 40:30–31

For I know the thoughts that I think toward you, says the LORD, thoughts of peace, and not of evil, to give you an expected end.
                                                       JEREMIAH 29:11

And not only so, but we glory in tribulations also: knowing that tribulation works patience. ROMANS 5:3

But if we hope for that we see not, then do we with patience wait for it. ROMANS 8:25

Strengthened with all might, according to His glorious power, to all patience and longsuffering with joyfulness. COLOSSIANS 1:11

And the Lord direct your hearts into the love of God, and into the patient waiting for Christ. 2 THESSALONIANS 3:5

But let patience have her perfect work, that you may be perfect and entire, wanting nothing. JAMES 1:4

The Lord is not slack concerning His promise, as some men count slackness; but is long-suffering to us-ward, not willing that any should perish, but that all should come to repentance. 2 PETER 3:9

INSIGHTS ON FAITH FROM SMITH WIGGLESWORTH

The baptism in the Holy Spirit is the essential power in the body that will bring rest from all your weariness and give you a hopeful expectation that each day may be the day we go up with Him.

❦

There is a way that God establishes. In our human planning, we may experience blessings of a kind, but we also undergo trials, hardships, and barrenness that God would have kept from us if we had followed His way. I realize through the anointing of the Holy Spirit that there is a freshness, a glow, a security in God where you can know that God is with you all the time. There is a place to reach where all that God has for us can flow through us to a needy world all the time: *"For as the heavens are higher than the earth, so are My ways higher than your ways, and My thoughts than your thoughts"* (Isa. 55:9).

❦

It is the Spirit that works in us all these divine plans so that He may build us on the foundations of the living Word, which lives, which always quickens and moves. Builds high, higher, higher, into and with love. It is always in a higher sense because God has no lower means.

KINDNESS

But the stranger that dwells with you shall be to you as one born among you, and you shall love him as yourself; for you were strangers in the land of Egypt: I am the LORD your God.

LEVITICUS 19:34

He that has pity upon the poor lends to the LORD; and that which he has given will He pay him again. PROVERBS 19:17

He that follows after righteousness and mercy finds life, righteousness, and honor. PROVERBS 21:21

She opens her mouth with wisdom; and in her tongue is the law of kindness. PROVERBS 31:26

He has showed you, O man, what is good; and what does the LORD require of you, but to do justly, and to love mercy, and to walk humbly with your God? MICAH 6:8

Blessed are the merciful: for they shall obtain mercy.

MATTHEW 5:7

Then shall the King say to them on His right hand, Come, you blessed of My Father, inherit the kingdom prepared for you from the foundation of the world: for I was hungry, and you gave Me meat: I was thirsty, and you gave Me drink: I was a stranger, and you took Me in: naked, and you clothed Me: I was sick, and you visited Me: I was in prison, and you came to Me.

MATTHEW 25:34–36

But love you your enemies, and do good, and lend, hoping for nothing again; and your reward shall be great, and you shall be the children of the Highest: for He is kind to the unthankful and to the evil.   LUKE 6:35

I have showed you all things, how that so laboring you ought to support the weak, and to remember the words of the Lord Jesus, how He said, It is more blessed to give than to receive.

ACTS 20:35

Behold therefore the goodness and severity of God: on them which fell, severity; but toward you, goodness, if you continue in His goodness: otherwise you also shall be cut off.   ROMANS 11:22

Let love be without dissimulation. Abhor that which is evil; cling to that which is good. Be kindly affectioned one to another with brotherly love; in honor preferring one another; not slothful in business; fervent in spirit; serving the Lord; rejoicing in hope; patient in tribulation; continuing instant in prayer; distributing to the necessity of saints; given to hospitality. ROMANS 12:9–13

Now the God of patience and consolation grant you to be like-minded one toward another according to Christ Jesus.
ROMANS 15:5

Put on therefore, as the elect of God, holy and beloved, bowels of mercies, kindness, humbleness of mind, meekness, longsuffering.
COLOSSIANS 3:12

Pure religion and undefiled before God and the Father is this, to visit the fatherless and widows in their affliction, and to keep himself unspotted from the world. JAMES 1:27

Finally, be you all of one mind, having compassion one of another, love as brethren, be pitiful, be courteous: not rendering evil for evil, or railing for railing: but contrariwise blessing; knowing that you are thereto called, that you should inherit a blessing.
1 PETER 3:8–9

FAITHFULNESS

And the Lord passed by before him, and proclaimed, The Lord, The Lord God, merciful and gracious, longsuffering, and abundant in goodness and truth. Exodus 34:6

Know therefore that the Lord your God, He is God, the faithful God, which keeps covenant and mercy with them that love Him and keep His commandments to a thousand generations. Deuteronomy 7:9

But You, O Lord, are a shield for me; my glory, and the lifter up of my head. Psalm 3:3

O love the Lord, all you His saints: for the Lord preserves the faithful, and plentifully rewards the proud doer. Psalm 31:23

I have not hid Your righteousness within my heart; I have declared Your faithfulness and Your salvation: I have not concealed Your lovingkindness and Your truth from the great congregation. Withhold not You Your tender mercies from me, O Lord: let Your lovingkindness and Your truth continually preserve me. Psalm 40:10–11

A faithful man shall abound with blessings: but he that makes haste to be rich shall not be innocent.   PROVERBS 28:20

No weapon that is formed against you shall prosper; and every tongue that shall rise against you in judgment you shall condemn. This is the heritage of the servants of the LORD, and their righteousness is of Me, says the LORD.   ISAIAH 54:17

And you shall seek Me, and find Me, when you shall search for Me with all your heart.   JEREMIAH 29:13

I will even betroth You to Me in faithfulness: and you shall know the LORD.   HOSEA 2:20

But the hour comes, and now is, when the true worshippers shall worship the Father in spirit and in truth: for the Father seeks such to worship Him.   JOHN 4:23

He that is faithful in that which is least is faithful also in much: and he that is unjust in the least is unjust also in much. If therefore you have not been faithful in the unrighteous mammon, who will commit to your trust the true riches? And if you have not been faithful in that which is another man's, who shall give you that which is your own?   LUKE 16:10–12

There has no temptation taken you but such as is common to man: but God is faithful, who will not suffer you to be tempted above that you are able; but will with the temptation also make a way to escape, that you may be able to bear it.

1 CORINTHIANS 10:13

So then they which be of faith are blessed with faithful Abraham.

GALATIANS 3:9

By faith Enoch was translated that he should not see death; and was not found, because God had translated him: for before his translation he had this testimony, that he pleased God. But without faith it is impossible to please Him: for he that comes to God must believe that He is, and that He is a rewarder of them that diligently seek Him.

HEBREWS 11:5–6

Here is the patience of the saints: here are they that keep the commandments of God, and the faith of Jesus. And I heard a voice from heaven saying to me, Write, Blessed are the dead which die in the Lord from hereafter: Yea, says the Spirit, that they may rest from their labors; and their works do follow them.

REVELATION 14:12–13

INSIGHTS ON FAITH FROM SMITH WIGGLESWORTH

We are born of the Spirit, and nothing but the Spirit of God can feed that spiritual life. We must live in it, feed in it, walk in it, talk in it, and sleep in it. Hallelujah! We must always be in the Holy Spirit whether asleep or awake. There is a place for man in the Holy Spirit where God has him; he is lost to every man, but he is never lost to God. God can find him any time He wants him. Oh, hallelujah!

The Holy Spirit coming upon an individual changes him and fertilizes his spiritual life. What things are possible if we reach this place and remain in it, that is, abide in it! Only one thing is going to accomplish the purpose of God, which is to be filled with the Spirit. We must yield and submit until our bodies are saturated with God, so that, at any moment, God's will can be revealed. We need a great hunger and thirst for God.

GOODNESS

And He said, I will make all my goodness pass before you, and I will proclaim the name of the LORD before you; and will be gracious to whom I will be gracious, and will show mercy on whom I will show mercy.   EXODUS 33:19

Surely goodness and mercy shall follow me all the days of my life: and I will dwell in the house of the LORD for ever.   PSALM 23:6

I had fainted, unless I had believed to see the goodness of the LORD in the land of the living.   PSALM 27:13

Oh how great is Your goodness, which You have laid up for them that fear You; which You have wrought for them that trust in You before the sons of men!   PSALM 31:19

O taste and see that the LORD is good: blessed is the man that trusts in Him.   PSALM 34:8

Blessed is the man whom You choose, and cause to approach to You, that he may dwell in Your courts: we shall be satisfied with the goodness of Your house, even of Your holy temple.

PSALM 65:4

For the LORD *is good; His mercy is everlasting; and His truth endures to all generations.* PSALM 100:5

A good man out of the good treasure of the heart brings forth good things: and an evil man out of the evil treasure brings forth evil things. MATTHEW 12:35

And I myself also am persuaded of you, my brethren, that you also are full of goodness, filled with all knowledge, able also to admonish one another. ROMANS 15:14

As we have therefore opportunity, let us do good to all men, especially to them who are of the household of faith. GALATIANS 6:10

With good will doing service, as to the Lord, and not to men. EPHESIANS 6:7

Every good gift and every perfect gift is from above, and comes down from the Father of lights, with whom is no variableness, neither shadow of turning. JAMES 1:17

INSIGHTS ON FAITH FROM SMITH WIGGLESWORTH

When the Holy Spirit falls as He did at the beginning, He enlarges the hearts of all the people to live in the Spirit in such a way that there is new vision, new revelation, new equipping for service; new men are created. The baptism of the Holy Spirit means a new creation after the order of the Spirit.

When the Holy Spirit takes hold of you, you will no longer rack your brains or have sleepless nights when preparing your addresses; God will do it. You will have a self-contained library in the Holy Spirit. He has the last thoughts from heaven—the first thoughts for earth.

We must see to it that we are filled with the Holy Spirit's power and be careful not to rest in any gift. We must be careful not to choose, but to let God's Holy Spirit manage our lives. We must not smooth down and explain away, but rather *"stir up the gift"* (2 Tim. 1:6); we must allow God's Spirit to disturb us and disturb us and disturb us until we yield and yield and yield and the possibility in God's mind for us becomes an established fact in our lives, with the rivers in evidence meeting the needs of a dying world.

SELF-CONTROL

Blessed is the man that walks not in the counsel of the ungodly, nor stands in the way of sinners, nor sits in the seat of the scornful. PSALM 1:1

He that is slow to anger is better than the mighty; and he that rules his spirit than he that takes a city. PROVERBS 16:32

He that has no rule over his own spirit is like a city that is broken down, and without walls. PROVERBS 25:28

A fool utters all his mind: but a wise man keeps it in till afterwards. PROVERBS 29:11

Watch and pray, that you enter not into temptation: the spirit indeed is willing, but the flesh is weak. MATTHEW 26:41

For they that are after the flesh do mind the things of the flesh; but they that are after the Spirit the things of the Spirit. ROMANS 8:5

I beseech you therefore, brethren, by the mercies of God, that you present your bodies a living sacrifice, holy, acceptable to God, which is your reasonable service. And be not conformed to this world: but be you transformed by the renewing of your mind, that you may prove what is that good, and acceptable, and perfect, will of God. ROMANS 12:1–2

What? know you not that your body is the temple of the Holy Ghost which is in you, which you have of God, and you are not your own? For you are bought with a price: therefore glorify God in your body, and in your spirit, which are God's.

1 CORINTHIANS 6:19–20

For God has not given us the spirit of fear; but of power, and of love, and of a sound mind.   2 TIMOTHY 1:7

[Be] a lover of hospitality, a lover of good men, sober, just, holy, temperate.   TITUS 1:8

Blessed is the man that endures temptation: for when he is tried, he shall receive the crown of life, which the Lord has promised to them that love Him.   JAMES 1:12

And beside this, giving all diligence, add to your faith virtue; and to virtue knowledge; and to knowledge temperance; and to temperance patience; and to patience godliness.   2 PETER 1:5–6

INSIGHTS ON FAITH FROM SMITH WIGGLESWORTH

God has promised to fill us. You may be filled with the mighty power of God, and yet, in a way, you may not realize it; still, you may know that you are being used by a power apart from yourself, a power that keeps you from self-exhibition. Just as the sun by its mighty power brings certain resources to nature, I believe the power of God in the human soul, the power filling it with Himself, is capable, by living faith, of bringing about what otherwise could never be accomplished. May God by His Spirit prepare us for what He has to say.

⌇

The Holy Spirit is waiting for us. The Holy Spirit has come, and He will not return until the church goes to be with her Lord forever. So when I see people waiting, I know something is wrong. The Holy Spirit is revealing uncleanness, judging, hardness of heart, all impurity. Until the process of cleansing is complete, the Holy Spirit cannot come. But when the body is clean, sanctified, Jesus delights to fill us with His Holy Spirit. The Holy Spirit is preparing our bodies as temples for the Spirit, to be made like Jesus is.

INSIGHTS ON FAITH FROM SMITH WIGGLESWORTH

Every one of you, if you have faith, can "stir up the gift" within you. The Holy Spirit can be so manifested in you that you can speak in utterances with tongues as He gives you the ability, even though you may not have actually received the gift of tongues. And I believe that everybody baptized in the Holy Spirit has a right to allow the Spirit to have perfect control and to speak every day, morning, noon, and night, in this way.

⌣

If you would get to know your place in the Holy Spirit, it would save you from struggles and burdens and would relieve the whole situation. Get to know your place in the Holy Spirit, and God will bless you.

⌣

This is a new day also for those who have been baptized, for the Spirit is an unlimited source of power. He is in no way stationary. Nothing in God is stationary. God has no place for a person who is stationary. The man who is going to catch the fire, hold forth the truth, and always be on the watchtower, is the one who is going to be a beacon for all saints, having a light greater than he would have naturally. He must see that God's grace, God's life, and God's Spirit are a million times mightier than he.

"THE LORD WANTS YOU TO BE
IN A SIGNIFICANT PLACE IN WHICH
THE HOLY SPIRIT HAS SUCH CONTROL
OF YOUR INNER EYES THAT HE MAY
REVEAL THE FULLNESS OF THE LORD
OF LIFE UNTIL JESUS IS GLORIFIED
TREMENDOUSLY BY THE REVELATION
OF THE HOLY SPIRIT, UNTIL HE
BECOMES LORD OVER ALL THINGS:
YOUR AFFECTIONS, YOUR WILL,
YOUR PURPOSES, YOUR PLANS,
AND YOUR WISHES FOREVER."

—SMITH WIGGLESWORTH

4

THE GIFTS OF THE SPIRIT

GIFT OF WISDOM

With the ancient is wisdom; and in length of days understanding. With Him is wisdom and strength, He has counsel and understanding. JOB 12:12–13

For the Lord gives wisdom: out of His mouth comes knowledge and understanding. PROVERBS 2:6

When wisdom enters into your heart, and knowledge is pleasant to your soul; discretion shall preserve you, understanding shall keep you. PROVERBS 2:10–11

Happy is the man that finds wisdom, and the man that gets understanding. For the merchandise of it is better than the merchandise of silver, and the gain thereof than fine gold. She is more precious than rubies: and all the things you can desire are not to be compared to her. Length of days is in her right hand; and in her left hand riches and honor. Her ways are ways of pleasantness, and all her paths are peace. PROVERBS 3:13–17

Forsake her not, and she shall preserve you: love her, and she shall keep you. Wisdom is the principal thing; therefore get wisdom: and with all your getting get understanding.   PROVERBS 4:6–7

Give instruction to a wise man, and he will be yet wiser: teach a just man, and he will increase in learning. The fear of the Lord is the beginning of wisdom: and the knowledge of the holy is understanding. For by me your days shall be multiplied, and the years of your life shall be increased. If you be wise, you shall be wise for yourself: but if you scorn, you alone shall bear it.
                                                           PROVERBS 9:9–12

He that walks with wise men shall be wise: but a companion of fools shall be destroyed.   PROVERBS 13:20

The fear of the LORD is the instruction of wisdom; and before honor is humility.   PROVERBS 15:33

Through wisdom is a house built; and by understanding it is established: and by knowledge shall the chambers be filled with all precious and pleasant riches. A wise man is strong; yea, a man of knowledge increases strength. For by wise counsel you shall make your war: and in multitude of counsellors there is safety. Wisdom is too high for a fool: he opens not his mouth in the gate.
                                                           PROVERBS 24:3–7

Who is as the wise man? and who knows the interpretation of a thing? a man's wisdom makes his face to shine, and the boldness of his face shall be changed.　　　　ECCLESIASTES 8:1

Call to Me, and I will answer you, and show you great and mighty things, which you know not.　　　　JEREMIAH 33:3

For I will give you a mouth and wisdom, which all your adversaries shall not be able to gainsay nor resist.　　　　LUKE 21:15

See then that you walk circumspectly, not as fools, but as wise, redeeming the time, because the days are evil. Wherefore be you not unwise, but understanding what the will of the Lord is.
　　　　EPHESIANS 5:15–17

If any of you lack wisdom, let him ask of God, that gives to all men liberally, and upbraids not; and it shall be given him.　JAMES 1:5

But the wisdom that is from above is first pure, then peaceable, gentle, and easy to be entreated, full of mercy and good fruits, without partiality, and without hypocrisy.　　　　JAMES 3:17

INSIGHTS ON FAITH FROM SMITH WIGGLESWORTH

Brothers and sisters, do you want the Holy Spirit? We sing some hymns that speak of the breath of the Holy Spirit. In the Bible, we read that Jesus breathed upon His disciples, and they received the anointing in His breath (John 20:22). As people breathe in the Holy Spirit, they become so possessed with the power of God that they have no possessions in themselves. They simply fall into God, and God takes possession of everything—hands, feet, body, and tongue—for His glory.

⌒

The baptism of the Holy Ghost is for revelation. The baptism of the Holy Ghost is to take the things of Jesus and reveal them to us. The baptism of the Holy Ghost is to be a focus.

GIFT OF KNOWLEDGE

The fear of the Lord *is the beginning of knowledge: but fools despise wisdom and instruction.*   Proverbs 1:7

Wisdom is the principal thing; therefore get wisdom: and with all your getting get understanding.   Proverbs 4:7

Receive my instruction, and not silver; and knowledge rather than choice gold.   Proverbs 8:10

The heart of him that has understanding seeks knowledge: but the mouth of fools feeds on foolishness.   Proverbs 15:14

The heart of the prudent gets knowledge; and the ear of the wise seeks knowledge.   Proverbs 18:5

Also, that the soul be without knowledge, it is not good; and he that hastens with his feet sins.   Proverbs 19:2

So shall the knowledge of wisdom be to your soul: when you have found it, then there shall be a reward, and your expectation shall not be cut off.   Proverbs 24:14

Teach me good judgment and knowledge: for I have believed Your commandments.   Psalm 119:66

For the earth shall be filled with the knowledge of the glory of the
LORD, as the waters cover the sea.   HABAKKUK 2:14

That you might walk worthy of the Lord to all pleasing, being
fruitful in every good work, and increasing in the knowledge
of God; strengthened with all might, according to His glorious
power, to all patience and longsuffering with joyfulness.
                                              COLOSSIANS 1:10–11

In whom [God] are hid all the treasures of wisdom and knowledge.   COLOSSIANS 2:3

And beside this, giving all diligence, add to your faith virtue;
and to virtue knowledge; and to knowledge temperance; and to
temperance patience; and to patience godliness; and to godliness
brotherly kindness; and to brotherly kindness charity. For if these
things be in you, and abound, they make you that you shall neither be barren nor unfruitful in the knowledge of our Lord Jesus
Christ.   2 PETER 1:5–8

GIFT OF FAITH

And Jesus answering says to them, Have faith in God. For verily I say to you, That whosoever shall say to this mountain, Be you removed, and be you cast into the sea; and shall not doubt in his heart, but shall believe that those things which he says shall come to pass; he shall have whatsoever he says. Therefore I say to you, What things soever you desire, when you pray, believe that you receive them, and you shall have them. MARK 11:22–24

And the apostles said to the Lord, Increase our faith. LUKE 17:5

Therefore we conclude that a man is justified by faith without the deeds of the law. ROMANS 3:28

For we walk by faith, not by sight. 2 CORINTHIANS 5:7

For therein is the righteousness of God revealed from faith to faith: as it is written, The just shall live by faith. ROMANS 1:17

So then faith comes by hearing, and hearing by the word of God. ROMANS 10:17

INSIGHTS ON FAITH FROM SMITH WIGGLESWORTH

The Holy Ghost is the manifestation of God's Son. The manifestation of the revelation of God's Son by the Holy Ghost, the Holy Ghost, always revealing Him to us as divine, as so uniquely divine that He is in power of overcoming, He is in power of purity, He is in power of rising all the time. And the Holy Ghost is shed abroad in our hearts for the very purpose that we may know that that which is in us has to go on to development. It must not cease development. The Holy Ghost is there for creating development and for moving us out as the Lord would have us to be.

When you received the Holy Ghost, it is certain the Lord is pleased with where you got to, but it is not where you are going to. Every man is sanctified, but no man in this place has received sanctification who has not an increased sanctification.

There is a place where God, through the power of the Holy Spirit, reigns supreme in our lives. The Spirit reveals, unfolds, takes of the things of Christ and shows them to us (John 16:15), and prepares us to be more than a match for satanic forces.

GIFT OF FAITH

Knowing that a man is not justified by the works of the law, but by the faith of Jesus Christ, even we have believed in Jesus Christ, that we might be justified by the faith of Christ, and not by the works of the law: for by the works of the law shall no flesh be justified. GALATIANS 2:16

For you are all the children of God by faith in Christ Jesus. GALATIANS 3:26

For by grace are you saved through faith; and that not of yourselves: it is the gift of God. EPHESIANS 2:8

We give thanks to God and the Father of our Lord Jesus Christ, praying always for you, since we heard of your faith in Christ Jesus, and of the love which you have to all the saints, for the hope which is laid up for you in heaven, whereof you heard before in the word of the truth of the gospel. COLOSSIANS 1:3–5

Now faith is the substance of things hoped for, the evidence of things not seen. For by it the elders obtained a good report. HEBREWS 11:1–2

Looking to Jesus the author and finisher of our faith; who for the joy that was set before Him endured the cross, despising the shame, and is set down at the right hand of the throne of God.

HEBREWS 12:2

Yea, a man may say, You have faith, and I have works: show me your faith without your works, and I will show you my faith by my works.

JAMES 2:18

For whatsoever is born of God overcomes the world: and this is the victory that overcomes the world, even our faith.

1 JOHN 5:4

Wherein you greatly rejoice, though now for a season, if need be, you are in heaviness through manifold temptations: that the trial of your faith, being much more precious than of gold that perishes, though it be tried with fire, might be found to praise and honor and glory at the appearing of Jesus Christ: whom having not seen, you love; in whom, though now you see Him not, yet believing, you rejoice with joy unspeakable and full of glory: receiving the end of your faith, even the salvation of your souls.

1 PETER 1:6–9

GIFT OF HEALING

And said, If you will diligently hearken to the voice of the LORD your God, and will do that which is right in His sight, and will give ear to His commandments, and keep all His statutes, I will put none of these diseases upon you, which I have brought upon the Egyptians: for I am the LORD that heals you.

EXODUS 15:26

The LORD will strengthen him upon the bed of languishing: You will make all his bed in his sickness.   PSALM 41:3

Be not wise in your own eyes: fear the LORD, and depart from evil. It shall be health to your navel, and marrow to your bones.

PROVERBS 3:7–8

There is that speaks like the piercings of a sword: but the tongue of the wise is health.   PROVERBS 12:18

Behold, I will bring it health and cure, and I will cure them, and will reveal to them the abundance of peace and truth.

JEREMIAH 33:6

INSIGHTS ON FAITH FROM SMITH WIGGLESWORTH

This filling of the Spirit will make your life effective, so that even the people in the stores where you shop will want to leave your presence because they are brought under conviction.

╰───╮

You can hardly go to a place now where God is not pouring out His Spirit upon hungry hearts. God has promised to pour out His Spirit upon all flesh, and His promises never fail. Our Christ is risen. His salvation was not a thing done in a corner. Truly He was a man of glory who went to Calvary for us in order that He might free us from all that would mar and hinder, that He might transform us by His grace and bring us out from under the power of the enemy into the glorious power of God.

╰───╮

It is impossible to overestimate the importance of being filled with the Spirit. It is impossible for us to meet the conditions of the day, to *"walk in the light as He is in the light"* (1 John 1:7), to subdue kingdoms and work righteousness and bind the power of Satan, unless we are filled with the Holy Spirit.

GIFT OF HEALING

And Jesus went about all the cities and villages, teaching in their synagogues, and preaching the gospel of the kingdom, and healing every sickness and every disease among the people.

MATTHEW 9:35

But Simon's wife's mother lay sick of a fever, and anon they tell Him of her. And He came and took her by the hand, and lifted her up; and immediately the fever left her, and she ministered to them.

MARK 1:30–31

And all things, whatsoever you shall ask in prayer, believing, you shall receive.

MATTHEW 21:22

And He said to them, In what place soever you enter into a house, there abide till you depart from that place. And whosoever shall not receive you, nor hear you, when you depart from there, shake off the dust under your feet for a testimony against them. Verily I say to you, It shall be more tolerable for Sodom and Gomorrha in the day of judgment, than for that city. And they went out, and preached that men should repent. And they cast out many devils, and anointed with oil many that were sick, and healed them.

MARK 6:10–13

By stretching forth Your hand to heal; and that signs and wonders may be done by the name of Your holy child Jesus.   ACTS 4:30

And by the hands of the apostles were many signs and wonders wrought among the people; and they were all with one accord in Solomon's porch…. Insomuch that they brought forth the sick into the streets, and laid them on beds and couches, that at the least the shadow of Peter passing by might overshadow some of them. There came also a multitude out of the cities round about to Jerusalem, bringing sick folks, and them which were vexed with unclean spirits: and they were healed every one.

ACTS 5:12, 15–16

To another faith by the same Spirit; to another the gifts of healing by the same Spirit. 1 CORINTHIANS 12:9

Is any sick among you? let him call for the elders of the church; and let them pray over him, anointing him with oil in the name of the Lord: and the prayer of faith shall save the sick, and the Lord shall raise him up; and if he have committed sins, they shall be forgiven him. JAMES 5:14–15

Who His own self bore our sins in His own body on the tree, that we, being dead to sins, should live to righteousness: by whose stripes you were healed. 1 PETER 2:24

GIFT OF MIRACLES

You are the God that does wonders: You have declared Your strength among the people.   PSALM 77:14

Seek the LORD, and His strength: seek His face evermore. Remember His marvelous works that He has done; His wonders, and the judgments of His mouth.   PSALM 105:4–5

He sent His word, and healed them, and delivered them from their destructions.   PSALM 107:20

And Jesus said to them, Because of your unbelief: for verily I say to you, If you have faith as a grain of mustard seed, you shall say to this mountain, Remove here to yonder place; and it shall remove; and nothing shall be impossible to you.
          MATTHEW 17:20

Believe Me that I am in the Father, and the Father in Me: or else believe Me for the very works' sake. Verily, verily, I say to you, He that believes on Me, the works that I do shall he do also; and greater works than these shall he do; because I go to My Father.
          JOHN 14:11–12

INSIGHTS ON FAITH FROM SMITH WIGGLESWORTH

We can never be filled with the Holy Spirit as long as there is any human craving for our own wills. Selfishness must be destroyed.

~

This should teach us that there is a need for every one of us to be filled with the Spirit of God. It is not sufficient just to have a touch of God or to usually have a desire for God. There is only one thing that will meet the needs of the people today, and that is to be immersed in the life of God—God taking you and filling you with His Spirit, until you live right in God, and God lives in you, so that *"whether you eat or drink, or whatever you do,"* it will all be for the *"glory of God"* (1 Cor. 10:31).

GIFT OF MIRACLES

And fear came upon every soul: and many wonders and signs were done by the apostles.　　　　　　　　　ACTS 2:43

By stretching forth Your hand to heal; and that signs and wonders may be done by the name of Your holy child Jesus.　　ACTS 4:30

Through mighty signs and wonders, by the power of the Spirit of God; so that from Jerusalem, and round about to Illyricum, I have fully preached the gospel of Christ.　　　ROMANS 15:19

Truly the signs of an apostle were wrought among you in all patience, in signs, and wonders, and mighty deeds.
2 CORINTHIANS 12:12

How shall we escape, if we neglect so great salvation; which at the first began to be spoken by the Lord, and was confirmed to us by them that heard Him; God also bearing them witness, both with signs and wonders, and with divers miracles, and gifts of the Holy Ghost, according to His own will?　　　HEBREWS 2:3–4

GIFT OF PROPHECY

And He said, Hear now My words: If there be a prophet among you, I the Lord will make Myself known to him in a vision, and will speak to him in a dream.   Numbers 12:6

I will raise them up a Prophet from among their brethren, like to you, and will put My words in his mouth; and he shall speak to them all that I shall command him. And it shall come to pass, that whosoever will not hearken to My words which he shall speak in My name, I will require it of him.   Deuteronomy 18:18–19

And it shall come to pass afterward, that I will pour out My Spirit upon all flesh; and your sons and your daughters shall prophesy, your old men shall dream dreams, your young men shall see visions: and also upon the servants and upon the handmaids in those days will I pour out My Spirit.   Joel 2:28–29

And it shall come to pass in the last days, says God, I will pour out of My Spirit upon all flesh: and your sons and your daughters shall prophesy, and your young men shall see visions, and your old men shall dream dreams.   Acts 2:17

And He gave some, apostles; and some, prophets; and some, evangelists; and some, pastors and teachers.   Ephesians 4:11

Now there are diversities of gifts, but the same Spirit.... And there are diversities of operations, but it is the same God which works all in all. But the manifestation of the Spirit is given to every man to profit withal.   1 CORINTHIANS 12:4, 6–7

And though I have the gift of prophecy, and understand all mysteries, and all knowledge; and though I have all faith, so that I could remove mountains, and have not charity, I am nothing.
1 CORINTHIANS 13:2

Follow after charity, and desire spiritual gifts, but rather that you may prophesy.   1 CORINTHIANS 14:1

But he that prophesies speaks to men to edification, and exhortation, and comfort.   1 CORINTHIANS 14:3

Quench not the Spirit. Despise not prophesyings. Prove all things; hold fast that which is good.   1 THESSALONIANS 5:19–21

But the anointing which you have received of Him abides in you, and you need not that any man teach you: but as the same anointing teaches you of all things, and is truth, and is no lie, and even as it has taught you, you shall abide in Him.   1 JOHN 2:27

INSIGHTS ON FAITH FROM SMITH WIGGLESWORTH

You must understand that God wants you to be continually in the place of prophecy, for everyone who has received the Holy Spirit has a right to prophesy. In 1 Corinthians 14:31, we read, *"You can all prophesy one by one."* Now prophecy is far in advance of speaking in tongues, except when you have the interpretation of the speaking in tongues, and then God gives an equivalent to prophecy. In verse 13, we read, *"Let him who speaks in a tongue pray that he may interpret."*

The Holy Spirit wants you to stir up your faith to believe that this word is true—that you have the anointing and that the anointing abides. As you rise up in the morning, believe this wonderful truth; and as you yield to the Spirit's presence and power, you will find yourself speaking to God in the Spirit, and you will find that you are personally being edified by doing this.

GIFT OF DISCERNING SPIRITS

Beware of false prophets, which come to you in sheep's clothing, but inwardly they are ravening wolves. MATTHEW 7:15

Judge not according to the appearance, but judge righteous judgment. JOHN 7:24

But he that is spiritual judges all things, yet he himself is judged of no man. For who has known the mind of the Lord, that he may instruct Him? but we have the mind of Christ. 1 CORINTHIANS 2:15–16

Wherefore I give you to understand, that no man speaking by the Spirit of God calls Jesus accursed: and that no man can say that Jesus is the Lord, but by the Holy Ghost. 1 CORINTHIANS 12:3

But the manifestation of the Spirit is given to every man to profit withal. For to one is given by the Spirit the word of wisdom; to another the word of knowledge by the same Spirit; to another faith by the same Spirit; to another the gifts of healing by the same Spirit; to another the working of miracles; to another prophecy; to another discerning of spirits; to another divers kinds of tongues; to another the interpretation of tongues: but all these works that one and the selfsame Spirit, dividing to every man severally as He will. 1 CORINTHIANS 12:7–11

For if he that comes preaches another Jesus, whom we have not preached, or if you receive another spirit, which you have not received, or another gospel, which you have not accepted, you might well bear with him. 2 CORINTHIANS 11:4

Be you therefore followers of God, as dear children.

EPHESIANS 5:1

Prove all things; hold fast that which is good.

1 THESSALONIANS 5:21

For the word of God is quick, and powerful, and sharper than any two-edged sword, piercing even to the dividing asunder of soul and spirit, and of the joints and marrow, and is a discerner of the thoughts and intents of the heart. HEBREWS 4:12

Beloved, believe not every spirit, but try the spirits whether they are of God: because many false prophets are gone out into the world. Hereby know you the Spirit of God: every spirit that confesses that Jesus Christ is come in the flesh is of God: and every spirit that confesses not that Jesus Christ is come in the flesh is not of God: and this is that spirit of antichrist, whereof you have heard that it should come; and even now already is it in the world.

1 JOHN 4:1–3

GIFT OF TONGUES

And these signs shall follow them that believe; in My name shall they cast out devils; they shall speak with new tongues; they shall take up serpents; and if they drink any deadly thing, it shall not hurt them; they shall lay hands on the sick, and they shall recover.   MARK 16:17–18

And when the day of Pentecost was fully come, they were all with one accord in one place. And suddenly there came a sound from heaven as of a rushing mighty wind, and it filled all the house where they were sitting. And there appeared to them cloven tongues like as of fire, and it sat upon each of them. And they were all filled with the Holy Ghost, and began to speak with other tongues, as the Spirit gave them utterance.   ACTS 2:1–4

Now when this was noised abroad, the multitude came together, and were confounded, because that every man heard them speak in his own language.   ACTS 2:6

Then Peter said to them, Repent, and be baptized every one of you in the name of Jesus Christ for the remission of sins, and you shall receive the gift of the Holy Ghost.   ACTS 2:38

INSIGHTS ON FAITH FROM SMITH WIGGLESWORTH

How important it is that we have the manifestation of "the word of knowledge" in our midst. The same Spirit who brings forth the word of wisdom brings forth the word of knowledge. The revelation of the mysteries of God comes by the Spirit, and we must have a supernatural word of knowledge in order to convey to others the things that the Spirit of God has revealed. The Spirit of God reveals Christ in all His wonderful fullness, and He shows Him to us from the beginning to the end of the Scriptures.

⌒

Yes, there is a power, a blessing, an assurance, a rest in the presence of the Holy Spirit. You can feel His presence and know that He is with you. You do not need to spend an hour without this inner knowledge of His holy presence. With His power upon you, there can be no failure. You are above par all the time.

GIFT OF TONGUES

When they heard this, they were baptized in the name of the Lord Jesus. And when Paul had laid his hands upon them, the Holy Ghost came on them; and they spoke with tongues, and prophesied. ACTS 19:5–6

For he that speaks in an unknown tongue speaks not to men, but to God: for no man understands him; howbeit in the spirit he speaks mysteries. 1 CORINTHIANS 14:2

He that speaks in an unknown tongue edifies himself; but he that prophesies edifies the church. 1 CORINTHIANS 14:4

For if I pray in an unknown tongue, my spirit prays, but my understanding is unfruitful. What is it then? I will pray with the spirit, and I will pray with the understanding also: I will sing with the spirit, and I will sing with the understanding also. Else when you shall bless with the spirit, how shall he that occupies the room of the unlearned say Amen at your giving of thanks, seeing he understands not what you say? For you verily give thanks well, but the other is not edified. I thank my God, I speak with tongues more than you all: yet in the church I had rather speak five words with my understanding, that by my voice I might teach others also, than ten thousand words in an unknown tongue. 1 CORINTHIANS 14:14–19

GIFT OF INTERPRETATION OF TONGUES

Whom shall He teach knowledge? and whom shall He make to understand doctrine? them that are weaned from the milk, and drawn from the breasts. For precept must be upon precept, precept upon precept; line upon line, line upon line; here a little, and there a little.   ISAIAH 28:9–10

However when He, the Spirit of truth, is come, He will guide you into all truth: for He shall not speak of Himself; but whatsoever He shall hear, that shall He speak: and He will show you things to come.   JOHN 16:13

For to one is given by the Spirit the word of wisdom; to another the word of knowledge by the same Spirit; to another faith by the same Spirit; to another the gifts of healing by the same Spirit; to another the working of miracles; to another prophecy; to another discerning of spirits; to another divers kinds of tongues; to another the interpretation of tongues.   1 CORINTHIANS 12:8–10

Wherefore let him that speaks in an unknown tongue pray that he may interpret.   1 CORINTHIANS 14:13

I would that you all spoke with tongues but rather that you prophesied: for greater is he that prophesies than he that speaks with tongues, except he interpret, that the church may receive edifying.   1 CORINTHIANS 14:5

How is it then, brethren? when you come together, every one of you has a psalm, has a doctrine, has a tongue, has a revelation, has an interpretation. Let all things be done to edifying. If any man speak in an unknown tongue, let it be by two, or at the most by three, and that by course; and let one interpret. But if there be no interpreter, let him keep silence in the church; and let him speak to himself, and to God.   1 CORINTHIANS 14: 26–28

Let all things be done decently and in order.
                                                        1 CORINTHIANS 14:40

And the angel said to me, Wherefore did you marvel? I will tell you the mystery of the woman, and of the beast that carries her, which has the seven heads and ten horns.   REVELATION 17:7

INSIGHTS ON FAITH FROM SMITH WIGGLESWORTH

When you receive the Holy Spirit, you receive God's gift, in whom are all the gifts of the Spirit.

～

There is a big difference between a pump and a spring. The law is a pump; the baptism in the Holy Spirit is a spring. The old pump gets out of order; the parts wear out, and the well runs dry. *"The letter kills"* (2 Cor. 3:6). But the spring is ever bubbling up, and there is a ceaseless flow direct from the throne of God. There is life.

～

The baptism of the Spirit is for the purpose of making us sons of God with power. (See Romans 1:4.) We will be conscious of our human limitations, but we will not limit the Holy One who has come to dwell within us. We must believe that since the Holy Spirit has come upon us, we are indeed sons of God with power. Never say "I can't." *"All things are possible to him who believes"* (Mark 9:23). Launch out into the deep and believe that God has His all for you and that you can do all things through Him who strengthens you (Phil 4:13).

"MANY PEOPLE THINK THAT GOD MAKES A DISTINCTION BETWEEN US AND THOSE WHO LIVED AT THE BEGINNING OF THE CHURCH. BUT THEY HAVE NO SCRIPTURE FOR THIS. WHEN ANYONE RECEIVES THE GIFT OF THE HOLY SPIRIT, THERE WILL ASSUREDLY BE NO DIFFERENCE BETWEEN HIS EXPERIENCE TODAY AND WHAT WAS GIVEN ON THE DAY OF PENTECOST."

—SMITH WIGGLESWORTH

5

POWER OF THE HOLY SPIRIT

MIGHT OF THE SPIRIT

And when he came to the den, he cried with a lamentable voice to Daniel: and the king spoke and said to Daniel, O Daniel, servant of the living God, is your God, whom you serve continually, able to deliver you from the lions? DANIEL 6:20

And such as do wickedly against the covenant shall he corrupt by flatteries: but the people that do know their God shall be strong, and do exploits. DANIEL 11:32

Restore to me the joy of Your salvation; and uphold me with Your free spirit. PSALM 51:12

And I say also to you, that you are Peter, and upon this rock I will build my church; and the gates of hell shall not prevail against it. MATTHEW 16:18

If you then, being evil, know how to give good gifts to your children: how much more shall your heavenly Father give the Holy Spirit to them that ask Him?　　　　　　　　　　LUKE 11:13

And, behold, I send the promise of My Father upon you: but tarry you in the city of Jerusalem, until you be endued with power from on high.　　　　　　　　　　LUKE 24:49

And when He had said this, He breathed on them, and says to them, Receive you the Holy Ghost.　　　　　　　　JOHN 20:22

What? know you not that your body is the temple of the Holy Ghost which is in you, which you have of God, and you are not your own?　　　　　　　　　　1 CORINTHIANS 6:19

Casting down imaginations, and every high thing that exalts itself against the knowledge of God, and bringing into captivity every thought to the obedience of Christ.　　　　2 CORINTHIANS 10:5

This is a faithful saying, and worthy of all acceptation, that Christ Jesus came into the world to save sinners; of whom I am chief.　　　　　　　　　　1 TIMOTHY 1:15

PENTECOSTAL POWER

And these signs shall follow them that believe; in My name shall they cast out devils; they shall speak with new tongues; they shall take up serpents; and if they drink any deadly thing, it shall not hurt them; they shall lay hands on the sick, and they shall recover.   MARK 16:17–18

Nevertheless I tell you the truth; it is expedient for you that I go away: for if I go not away, the Comforter will not come to you; but if I depart, I will send Him to you.   JOHN 16:7

Until the day in which He was taken up, after that He through the Holy Ghost had given commandments to the apostles whom He had chosen: to whom also He showed Himself alive after His passion by many infallible proofs, being seen of them forty days, and speaking of the things pertaining to the kingdom of God: and, being assembled together with them, commanded them that they should not depart from Jerusalem, but wait for the promise of the Father, which, says He, you have heard of Me. For John truly baptized with water; but you shall be baptized with the Holy Ghost not many days from now.   ACTS 1:2–5

And believers were the more added to the Lord, multitudes both of men and women. Insomuch that they brought forth the sick into the streets, and laid them on beds and couches, that at the least the shadow of Peter passing by might overshadow some of them.
                                                                    ACTS 5:14–15

INSIGHTS ON FAITH FROM SMITH WIGGLESWORTH

If you are a businessman, you need to be baptized in the Holy Spirit. For any kind of business, you need to know the power of the Holy Spirit, because if you are not baptized with the Holy Spirit, Satan has a tremendous power to interfere with the progress of your life. If you come into the baptism of the Holy Spirit, there is a new realm for your business.

⌇

The man who is baptized in the Holy Spirit is baptized into a new order altogether. You cannot ever be ordinary after that. You are on an extraordinary plane; you are brought into line with the mind of God. You have come into touch with ideals in every way.

⌇

When the Holy Spirit is allowed full reign over the operation of human life, He always works out divine wisdom. And when He gets perfect control of a life, the divine source flows through so that all the people may receive edification in the Spirit.

PENTECOSTAL POWER

When they heard this, they were baptized in the name of the Lord Jesus. And when Paul had laid his hands upon them, the Holy Ghost came on them; and they spoke with tongues, and prophesied. ACTS 19:5–6

And the evil spirit answered and said, Jesus I know, and Paul I know; but who are you? ACTS 19:15

Nay, in all these things we are more than conquerors through Him that loved us. ROMANS 8:37

So that you come behind in no gift; waiting for the coming of our Lord Jesus Christ. 1 CORINTHIANS 1:7

But the manifestation of the Spirit is given to every man to profit withal. 1 CORINTHIANS 12:7

Always bearing about in the body the dying of the Lord Jesus, that the life also of Jesus might be made manifest in our body. 2 CORINTHIANS 4:10

And has put all things under His feet, and gave Him to be the head over all things to the church. EPHESIANS 1:22

Who being the brightness of His glory, and the express image of His person, and upholding all things by the word of His power, when He had by Himself purged our sins, sat down on the right hand of the Majesty on high.   HEBREWS 1:3

And of the angels He said, Who makes His angels spirits, and His ministers a flame of fire.   HEBREWS 1:7

Beloved, think it not strange concerning the fiery trial which is to try you, as though some strange thing happened to you.

1 PETER 4:12

You are of God, little children, and have overcome them: because greater is He that is in you, than he that is in the world.

1 JOHN 4:4

These shall make war with the Lamb, and the Lamb shall overcome them: for He is Lord of lords, and Kings of kings: and they that are with Him are called, and chosen, and faithful.

REVELATION 17:14

POWER TO PRESS THROUGH

That it might be fulfilled which was spoken by Isaiah the prophet, saying, Himself took our infirmities, and bore our sicknesses.

MATTHEW 8:17

And all things, whatsoever you shall ask in prayer, believing, you shall receive. MATTHEW 21:22

And immediately many were gathered together, insomuch that there was no room to receive them, no, not so much as about the door: and He preached the word to them. MARK 2:2

When Jesus saw their faith, He said to the sick of the palsy, Son, your sins be forgiven you. MARK 2:5

And immediately he arose, took up the bed, and went forth before them all; insomuch that they were all amazed, and glorified God, saying, We never saw it on this fashion. MARK 2:12

For the Son of man is come to seek and to save that which was lost. LUKE 19:10

INSIGHTS ON FAITH FROM SMITH WIGGLESWORTH

For when I speak about the Holy Spirit, it is always with reference to revelations of Jesus. The Holy Spirit is only the Revealer of the mighty Christ who has everything for us so that we may never know any weakness. All limitations are gone. And you are now in a place where God has taken the ideal and moved you on with His own velocity, which has a speed beyond all human mind and thought. Glory to God!

Our minds and our bodies—our whole position through the eternal Spirit—always have to be on the ascending position. To descend is to be conformed. To ascend is to be transformed. In this transforming condition, we may, by the power of the Spirit, as God gives us revelation, be lifted up into a very blessed state of fellowship with God, of power with God. And in that place of power with God, we will have power over everything else, for to have all power over the earth, we must first have power with God.

POWER TO PRESS THROUGH

For all the promises of God in Him are yea, and in Him Amen, to the glory of God by us. 2 CORINTHIANS 1:20

Therefore if any man be in Christ, he is a new creature: old things are passed away; behold, all things are become new.
2 CORINTHIANS 5:17

To me, who am less than the least of all saints, is this grace given, that I should preach among the Gentiles the unsearchable riches of Christ. EPHESIANS 3:8

For we have not an high priest which cannot be touched with the feeling of our infirmities; but was in all points tempted like as we are, yet without sin. HEBREWS 4:15

Who in the days of His flesh, when He had offered up prayers and supplications with strong crying and tears to Him that was able to save Him from death, and was heard in that He feared.
HEBREWS 5:7

Draw near to God, and He will draw near to you. Cleanse your hands, you sinners; and purify your hearts, you double minded.
JAMES 4:8

POWER OF THE TONGUE

I called upon the LORD *in distress: the* LORD *answered me, and set me in a large place.*
PSALM 118:5

Set a watch, O LORD, *before my mouth; keep the door of my lips.*
PSALM 141:3

In the multitude of words there wants not sin: but he that refrains his lips is wise.
PROVERBS 10:19

There is that speaks like the piercings of a sword: but the tongue of the wise is health.
PROVERBS 12:18

A wholesome tongue is a tree of life: but perverseness therein is a breach in the spirit.
PROVERBS 15:4

He that has knowledge spares his words: and a man of understanding is of an excellent spirit.
PROVERBS 17:27

Death and life are in the power of the tongue: and they that love it shall eat the fruit thereof.
PROVERBS 18:21

But I say to you, That every idle word that men shall speak, they shall give account thereof in the day of judgment. For by your words you shall be justified, and by your words you shall be condemned.
MATTHEW 12:36–37

INSIGHTS ON FAITH FROM SMITH WIGGLESWORTH

Spiritual power will not have human attainment. The man that is living in the Spirit will not turn aside to please anybody. The man that is filled with the Spirit it is going on with God all the time, and he will cease from his own works.

~

The Holy Spirit coming upon an individual is capable of changing him, fertilizing his spiritual life, and filling him with such power and grace that he wouldn't be able to say that anything was impossible but that all things are possible with God (Matt. 19:26). What could happen, what is possible, if we reach this place and stay in it—if we abide in it? Some people have an idea that they have to be doing something. I implore you, by the power of the Holy Spirit, that you see that there is only one thing that is going to accomplish the purposes of God, and that is being in the Spirit. I don't care how dry the land is. I don't care how thirsty the land is. I don't care how many or how few vessels are available. I implore you, in the name of Jesus, to keep in the Spirit. That's the secret.

POWER OF THE TONGUE

With all lowliness and meekness, with longsuffering, forbearing one another in love.

EPHESIANS 4:2

If any man among you seem to be religious, and bridles not his tongue, but deceives his own heart, this man's religion is vain.

JAMES 1:26

For in many things we offend all. If any man offend not in word, the same is a perfect man, and able also to bridle the whole body.

JAMES 3:2

Even so the tongue is a little member, and boasts great things. Behold, how great a matter a little fire kindles! And the tongue is a fire, a world of iniquity: so is the tongue among our members, that it defiles the whole body, and sets on fire the course of nature; and it is set on fire of hell. For every kind of beasts, and of birds, and of serpents, and of things in the sea, is tamed, and has been tamed of mankind: but the tongue can no man tame; it is an unruly evil, full of deadly poison.

JAMES 3:5–8

For he that will love life, and see good days, let him refrain his tongue from evil, and his lips that they speak no guile.

1 PETER 3:10

POWER TO DO MIRACLES

*Behold, I am the L*ORD*, the God of all flesh: is there any thing too hard for Me?*   JEREMIAH 32:27

Jesus said to him, If you can believe, all things are possible to him that believes.   MARK 9:23

And they went forth, and preached every where, the Lord working with them, and confirming the word with signs following. Amen.   MARK 16:20

Judas says to Him, not Iscariot, Lord, how is it that You will manifest Yourself to us, and not to the world?   JOHN 14:22

And by the hands of the apostles were many signs and wonders wrought among the people; and they were all with one accord in Solomon's porch.   ACTS 5:12

And Stephen, full of faith and power, did great wonders and miracles among the people.   ACTS 6:8

And He said to me, My grace is sufficient for you: for My strength is made perfect in weakness. Most gladly therefore will I rather glory in my infirmities, that the power of Christ may rest upon me.   2 CORINTHIANS 12:9

INSIGHTS ON FAITH FROM SMITH WIGGLESWORTH

Before Jesus went to heaven, He told His disciples that they would receive the power of the Holy Spirit upon them, too (Acts 1:8). Thus, through them, His gracious ministry would continue. This power of the Holy Spirit was not only for a few apostles, but even for those who were afar off, even as many as our God would call (Acts 2:39), even for us way down in this century.

∽

There is no stopping point in the Spirit-filled life. We begin at the Cross, the place of disgrace, shame, and death, and that very death brings the power of resurrection life. Then, being filled with the Holy Spirit, we go on *"from glory to glory"* (2 Cor. 3:18). Let us not forget that possessing the baptism in the Holy Spirit means that there must be an ever increasing holiness.

∽

The Spirit of God can change our nature. God is the Creator. His Word is creative, and if you believe, His creative power can change your whole nature. You can become *"children of God"* (John 1:12). You cannot reach this altitude of faith alone. No man can keep himself. The all-powerful God spreads His covering over you, saying, *"If you can believe, all things are possible to him who believes"* (Mark 9:23).

POWER TO DO MIRACLES

Truly the signs of an apostle were wrought among you in all patience, in signs, and wonders, and mighty deeds.

2 CORINTHIANS 12:12

But covet earnestly the best gifts: and yet show I to you a more excellent way.

1 CORINTHIANS 12:31

And what is the exceeding greatness of His power to us-ward who believe, according to the working of His mighty power.

EPHESIANS 1:19

Now to Him that is able to do exceeding abundantly above all that we ask or think, according to the power that works in us.

EPHESIANS 3:20

I can do all things through Christ which strengthens me.

PHILIPPIANS 4:13

Wherefore I put you in remembrance that you stir up the gift of God, which is in you by the putting on of my hands.

2 TIMOTHY 1:6

All scripture is given by inspiration of God, and is profitable for doctrine, for reproof, for correction, for instruction in righteousness: that the man of God may be perfect, thoroughly furnished to all good works. 2 TIMOTHY 3:16–17

Neglect not the gift that is in you, which was given you by prophecy, with the laying on of the hands of the presbytery. 1 TIMOTHY 4:14

God also bearing them witness, both with signs and wonders, and with divers miracles, and gifts of the Holy Ghost, according to His own will? HEBREWS 2:4

Is any sick among you? let him call for the elders of the church; and let them pray over him, anointing him with oil in the name of the Lord: and the prayer of faith shall save the sick, and the Lord shall raise him up; and if he have committed sins, they shall be forgiven him. Confess your faults one to another, and pray one for another, that you may be healed. The effectual fervent prayer of a righteous man avails much. JAMES 5:14–16

According as His divine power has given to us all things that pertain to life and godliness, through the knowledge of Him that has called us to glory and virtue. 2 PETER 1:3

ABIDING IN POWER

I the LORD *search the heart, I try the reins, even to give every man according to his ways, and according to the fruit of his doings.*

JEREMIAH 17:10

So I prophesied as I was commanded: and as I prophesied, there was a noise, and behold a shaking, and the bones came together, bone to his bone.

EZEKIEL 37:7

And Jesus, when He was baptized, went up immediately out of the water: and, lo, the heavens were opened to Him, and he saw the Spirit of God descending like a dove, and lighting upon Him: and lo a voice from heaven, saying, This is My beloved Son, in whom I am well pleased.

MATTHEW 3:16–17

And when He had said this, He breathed on them, and says to them, Receive you the Holy Ghost.

JOHN 20:22

For it is God which works in you both to will and to do of His good pleasure.

PHILIPPIANS 2:13

And be not conformed to this world: but be you transformed by the renewing of your mind, that you may prove what is that good, and acceptable, and perfect, will of God.

ROMANS 12:2

INSIGHTS ON FAITH FROM SMITH WIGGLESWORTH

There are two sides to the baptism of the Holy Spirit. The first condition is that you possess the baptism; the second condition is that the baptism possesses you. The first has to happen before the second can occur. God can so manifest His divine power that all souls can possess, if they are eligible, this blessed infilling of the baptism of the Holy Spirit. There is no limit to it. It cannot be measured. It is without limit because God is behind it, in the middle of it, and through it.

⌒

The inward man instantly receives the Holy Spirit with great joy and blessedness. He cannot express it. It is beyond his expression. He received the power of the Spirit, which is the Word.

POWER TO BIND THE ENEMY

Your right hand, O Lord, is become glorious in power: your right hand, O Lord, has dashed in pieces the enemy. And in the greatness of your excellency You have overthrown them that rose up against You: You sent forth Your wrath, which consumed them as stubble. EXODUS 15:6–7

None is so fierce that dare stir him up: who then is able to stand before Me? JOB 41:10

You broke the heads of leviathan in pieces, and gave him to be meat to the people inhabiting the wilderness. PSALM 74:14

The Lord on high is mightier than the noise of many waters, yea, than the mighty waves of the sea. PSALM 93:4

Then they cry to the Lord in their trouble, and He brings them out of their distresses. He makes the storm a calm, so that the waves thereof are still. PSALM 107:28–29

In that day the Lord with His sore and great and strong sword shall punish leviathan the piercing serpent, even leviathan that crooked serpent; and He shall slay the dragon that is in the sea.

ISAIAH 27:1

Thus says the LORD, *which makes a way in the sea, and a path in the mighty waters.* ISAIAH 43:16

That says to the deep, Be dry, and I will dry up your rivers. ISAIAH 44:27

Speak, and say, Thus says the LORD *God; Behold, I am against you, Pharaoh king of Egypt, the great dragon that lies in the midst of its rivers, which has said, my river is my own, and I have made it for myself. But I will put hooks in your jaws, and I will cause the fish of your rivers to stick to your scales, and I will bring you up out of the midst of your rivers, and all the fish of your rivers shall stick to your scales. And I will leave you thrown into the wilderness, you and all the fish of your rivers: you shall fall upon the open fields; you shall not be brought together, nor gathered: I have given you for meat to the beasts of the field and to the fowls of the heaven.* EZEKIEL 29:3–5

Or else how can one enter into a strong man's house, and spoil his goods, except he first bind the strong man? and then he will spoil his house. MATTHEW 12:29

And I will give to you the keys of the kingdom of heaven: and whatsoever you shall bind on earth shall be bound in heaven: and whatsoever you shall loose on earth shall be loosed in heaven. MATTHEW 16:19

And these signs shall follow them that believe; in My name shall they cast out devils; they shall speak with new tongues.

MARK 16:17

Behold, I give to you power to tread on serpents and scorpions, and over all the power of the enemy: and nothing shall by any means hurt you.

LUKE 10:19

To open their eyes, and to turn them from darkness to light, and from the power of Satan to God, that they may receive forgiveness of sins, and inheritance among them which are sanctified by faith that is in Me.

ACTS 26:18

For God has not given us the spirit of fear; but of power, and of love, and of a sound mind.

2 TIMOTHY 1:7

Be sober, be vigilant; because your adversary the devil, as a roaring lion, walks about, seeking whom he may devour.

1 PETER 5:8

INSIGHTS ON FAITH FROM SMITH WIGGLESWORTH

The inward man receives the Holy Spirit instantly with great joy and blessedness. He cannot express it. Then the power of the Spirit, this breath of God, takes of the things of Jesus (see John 16:14–15) and sends forth as a river the utterances of the Spirit. Again, when the body is filled with joy, sometimes so inexpressible, and the joy is thrown on the canvas of the mind, the canvas of the mind has great power to move the operation of the tongue to bring out the very depths of the inward heart's power, love, and joy to us. By the same process, the Spirit, which is the breath of God, brings forth the manifestation of the glory.

〜

When you are in the Spirit and the dry bones surround you and barren conditions are all around you; when you think everything is exactly the opposite of your desires and you can see no deliverance by human power; then, knowing that your condition is known to God and that God wants men and women who are willing to submit and submit and yield and yield to the Holy Spirit until their bodies are saturated and soaked with God, you realize that God your Father has you in such a condition that, at any moment, He can reveal His will to you.

POWER OF THE BLOOD

And the blood shall be to you for a token upon the houses where you are: and when I see the blood, I will pass over you, and the plague shall not be upon you to destroy you, when I smite the land of Egypt.   EXODUS 12:13

For this is My blood of the new testament, which is shed for many for the remission of sins.   MATTHEW 26:28

Even as the Son of man came not to be ministered to, but to minister, and to give His life a ransom for many. MATTHEW 20:28

Whom God hath set forth to be a propitiation through faith in His blood, to declare His righteousness for the remission of sins that are past, through the forbearance of God.   ROMANS 3:25

When Jesus had lifted up Himself, and saw none but the woman, He said to her, Woman, where are those your accusers? has no man condemned you?   JOHN 8:10

Much more then, being now justified by His blood, we shall be saved from wrath through Him.   ROMANS 5:9

In whom we have redemption through His blood, the forgiveness of sins, according to the riches of His grace.   EPHESIANS 1:7

And, having made peace through the blood of His cross, by Him to reconcile all things to Himself; by Him, I say, whether they be things in earth, or things in heaven.   COLOSSIANS 1:20

Forasmuch then as the children are partakers of flesh and blood, He also Himself likewise took part of the same; that through death He might destroy him that had the power of death, that is, the devil.   HEBREWS 2:14

And their sins and iniquities will I remember no more.   HEBREWS 10:17

Having therefore, brethren, boldness to enter into the holiest by the blood of Jesus.   HEBREWS 10:19

You have not yet resisted to blood, striving against sin.   HEBREWS 12:4

And to Jesus the mediator of the new covenant, and to the blood of sprinkling, that speaks better things than that of Abel.   HEBREWS 12:24

Now the God of peace, that brought again from the dead our Lord Jesus, that great shepherd of the sheep, through the blood of the everlasting covenant, make you perfect in every good work to do His will, working in you that which is well-pleasing in His sight, through Jesus Christ; to whom be glory for ever and ever. Amen.

HEBREWS 13:20–21

Forasmuch as you know that you were not redeemed with corruptible things, as silver and gold, from your vain conversation received by tradition from your fathers; but with the precious blood of Christ, as of a lamb without blemish and without spot.

1 PETER 1:18–19

And I heard a loud voice saying in heaven, Now is come salvation, and strength, and the kingdom of our God, and the power of his Christ: for the accuser of our brethren is cast down, which accused them before our God day and night. And they overcame him by the blood of the Lamb, and by the word of their testimony; and they loved not their lives to the death.

REVELATION 12:10–11

INSIGHTS ON FAITH FROM SMITH WIGGLESWORTH

As you live in the Spirit, when you walk down the steps of your house, the devil will have to flee before you. You will be more than a conqueror over the devil (Rom. 8:37).

⌣

When you received the Holy Spirit, it is certain that the Lord was pleased with the place at which you had arrived, but it is not where you are going to. Every believer is sanctified, but no believer has received sanctification who does not also have an increased sanctification. There is no man being saved today who does not need to have an increased salvation, truth upon truth, *"line upon line"* (Isa. 28:10), knowing that he is ripe for heaven but that he is also going on to perfection. He is being changed *"from glory to glory"* (2 Cor. 3:18). The process is wonderful: being saved, being sanctified, being made ready every day!

⌣

The baptism of the Holy Spirit is essential for bringing into you a divine, holy fire that burns up all dross and quickens all purity, making you ablaze so that perfect love may continue. The baptism of the Holy Spirit and the baptism of fire are one and the same. The baptism is the infilling of the divine third person of the Trinity.

"OH, IF I COULD ONLY STIR YOU UP TO SEE THAT, AS YOU ARE FAITHFUL IN THE HUMBLEST ROLE, GOD CAN FILL YOU WITH HIS SPIRIT, MAKE YOU A CHOSEN VESSEL FOR HIMSELF, AND PROMOTE YOU TO A PLACE OF MIGHTY MINISTRY IN THE SALVATION OF SOULS AND IN THE HEALING OF THE SICK! NOTHING IS IMPOSSIBLE TO A PERSON FILLED WITH THE HOLY SPIRIT."

—SMITH WIGGLESWORTH

6

GOING DEEPER

THIRSTING FOR FULLNESS

You love righteousness, and hate wickedness: therefore God, Your God, has anointed You with the oil of gladness above Your fellows.   PSALM 45:7

But I say to you, That whosoever looks on a woman to lust after her has committed adultery with her already in his heart.
                                    MATTHEW 5:28

But as many as received Him, to them gave He power to become the sons of God, even to them that believe on His name.
                                    JOHN 1:12

Philip says to Him, Lord, show us the Father, and it sufficed us.
                                    JOHN 14:8

These things I have spoken to you, that in Me you might have peace. In the world you shall have tribulation: but be of good cheer; I have overcome the world.   JOHN 16:33

In the last day, that great day of the feast, Jesus stood and cried, saying, If any man thirst, let him come to Me, and drink. He that believes on Me, as the scripture has said, out of his belly shall flow rivers of living water. (But this spoke He of the Spirit, which they that believe on Him should receive: for the Holy Ghost was not yet given; because that Jesus was not yet glorified.) JOHN 7:37–39

And now I am no more in the world, but these are in the world, and I come to You. Holy Father, keep through Your own name those whom You have given Me, that they may be one, as We are.... I have given them Your word; and the world has hated them, because they are not of the world, even as I am not of the world. JOHN 17:11, 14

Now when they saw the boldness of Peter and John, and perceived that they were unlearned and ignorant men, they marveled; and they took knowledge of them, that they had been with Jesus. ACTS 4:13

For the law of the Spirit of life in Christ Jesus has made me free from the law of sin and death. ROMANS 8:2

The first man is of the earth, earthy; the second man is the Lord from heaven. 1 CORINTHIANS 15:47

For the flesh lusts against the Spirit, and the Spirit against the flesh: and these are contrary the one to the other: so that you cannot do the things that you would.   GALATIANS 5:17

For it is God which works in you both to will and to do of His good pleasure.   PHILIPPIANS 2:13

Yea doubtless, and I count all things but loss for the excellency of the knowledge of Christ Jesus my Lord: for whom I have suffered the loss of all things, and do count them but dung, that I may win Christ.   PHILIPPIANS 3:8

Forasmuch then as the children are partakers of flesh and blood, He also Himself likewise took part of the same; that through death He might destroy him that had the power of death, that is, the devil.   HEBREWS 2:14

But every man is tempted, when he is drawn away of his own lust, and enticed.   JAMES 1:14

You ask, and receive not, because you ask amiss, that you may consume it upon your lusts.   JAMES 4:3

Be patient therefore, brethren, to the coming of the Lord. Behold, the husbandman waits for the precious fruit of the earth, and has long patience for it, until he receive the early and latter rain.   JAMES 5:7

INSIGHTS ON FAITH FROM SMITH WIGGLESWORTH

As you come closer to God, the Spirit reveals His holiness and shows us a new plan for the present and the future. The height and depth, the breadth and length of God's inheritance for us are truly wonderful.

❧

With the gifts of the Spirit should come the fruit of the Spirit. With wisdom we should have love, with knowledge we should have joy, and with faith we should have the fruit of peace. Faith is always accompanied by peace. Faith always rests. Faith laughs at impossibilities. Salvation is by faith, through grace, and "*it is the gift of God*" (Eph. 2:8).

❧

The power of God is beyond all our conception. The trouble is that we do not have the power of God in a full manifestation because of our finite thoughts, but as we go on and let God have His way, there is no limit to what our limitless God will do in response to a limitless faith. But you will never get anywhere unless you are in constant pursuit of all the power of God.

MINISTRY OF THE SPIRIT

I delight to do Your will, O my God: yea, Your law is within my heart. PSALM 40:8

Whosoever therefore shall humble himself as this little child, the same is greatest in the kingdom of heaven. MATTHEW 18:4

But Jesus said, Permit little children, and forbid them not, to come to Me: for of such is the kingdom of heaven. MATTHEW 19:14

And they were exceeding sorrowful, and began every one of them to say to Him, Lord, is it I? MATTHEW 26:22

For the law was given by Moses, but grace and truth came by Jesus Christ. JOHN 1:17

But the Comforter, which is the Holy Ghost, whom the Father will send in My name, He shall teach you all things, and bring all things to your remembrance, whatsoever I have said to you. JOHN 14:26

And one of them smote the servant of the high priest, and cut off his right ear. And Jesus answered and said, Suffer you thus far. And He touched his ear, and healed him. Then Jesus said to the chief priests, and captains of the temple, and the elders, which were come to Him, Be you come out, as against a thief, with swords and staves? LUKE 22:50–52

Therefore we are buried with Him by baptism into death: that like as Christ was raised up from the dead by the glory of the Father, even so we also should walk in newness of life.   ROMANS 6:4

I thank God through Jesus Christ our Lord. So then with the mind I myself serve the law of God; but with the flesh the law of sin.   ROMANS 7:25

For the kingdom of God is not in word, but in power.
                                                    1 CORINTHIANS 4:20

You are our epistle written in our hearts, known and read of all men. Forasmuch as you are manifestly declared to be the epistle of Christ ministered by us, written not with ink, but with the Spirit of the living God; not in tables of stone, but in fleshy tables of the heart.   2 CORINTHIANS 3:2–3

Not that we are sufficient of ourselves to think any thing as of ourselves; but our sufficiency is of God; who also has made us able ministers of the new testament; not of the letter, but of the Spirit: for the letter kills, but the Spirit gives life.
                                                    2 CORINTHIANS 3:5–6

Stand therefore, having your loins girt about with truth, and having on the breastplate of righteousness.

EPHESIANS 6:14

To whom God would make known what is the riches of the glory of this mystery among the Gentiles; which is Christ in you, the hope of glory.

COLOSSIANS 1:27

Because it is written, Be you holy; for I am holy.

1 PETER 1:16

That which was from the beginning, which we have heard, which we have seen with our eyes, which we have looked upon, and our hands have handled, of the Word of life.

1 JOHN 1:1

But the anointing which you have received of Him abides in you, and you need not that any man teach you: but as the same anointing teaches you of all things, and is truth, and is no lie, and even as it has taught you, you shall abide in Him.

1 JOHN 2:27

INSIGHTS ON FAITH FROM SMITH WIGGLESWORTH

I believe in the baptism of the Holy Spirit with the speaking in tongues, and I believe that every man who is baptized in the Holy Spirit will *"speak with other tongues, as the Spirit [gives him] utterance"* (Acts 2:4). I believe in the Holy Spirit. And if you are filled with the Spirit, you will be superabounding in life, and living waters will flow from you.

⟳

As we are filled with the Holy Spirit, God purposes that like our Lord, we should love righteousness and hate lawlessness. I see that there is a place for us in Christ Jesus where we are no longer under condemnation but where the heavens are always open to us. I see that God has a realm of divine life opening up to us where there are boundless possibilities, where there is limitless power, where there are untold resources, and where we have victory over all the power of the Devil.

⟳

I believe that, as we are filled with the desire to press on into this life of true holiness, desiring only the glory of God, nothing can hinder our true advancement.

IMMERSED IN THE SPIRIT

But know that the LORD has set apart him that is godly for Himself: the LORD will hear when I call to Him.   PSALM 4:3

They that sow in tears shall reap in joy.   PSALM 126:5

When a man's ways please the LORD, He makes even his enemies to be at peace with him.   PROVERBS 16:7

Can the Ethiopian change his skin, or the leopard his spots? then may you also do good, that are accustomed to do evil.
    JEREMIAH 13:23

And it shall come to pass afterward, that I will pour out My Spirit upon all flesh; and your sons and your daughters shall prophesy, your old men shall dream dreams, your young men shall see visions: and also upon the servants and upon the handmaids in those days will I pour out My Spirit.   JOEL 2:28–29

In that day shall there be upon the bells of the horses, HOLINESS TO THE LORD; and the pots in the LORD's house shall be like the bowls before the altar.   ZECHARIAH 14:20

Behold, I will send you Elijah the prophet before the coming of the great and dreadful day of the LORD: and he shall turn the heart of the fathers to the children, and the heart of the children to their fathers, lest I come and smite the earth with a curse.

MALACHI 4:5-6

I indeed have baptized you with water: but He shall baptize you with the Holy Ghost.

MARK 1:8

However when He, the Spirit of truth, is come, He will guide you into all truth: for He shall not speak of Himself; but whatsoever He shall hear, that shall He speak: and He will show you things to come. He shall glorify Me: for He shall receive of Mine, and shall show it to you. All things that the Father has are Mine: therefore said I, that He shall take of Mine, and shall show it to you.

JOHN 16:13–15

And he trembling and astonished said, Lord, what will You have me to do? And the Lord said to him, Arise, and go into the city, and it shall be told you what you must do.

ACTS 9:6

And when they found them not, they drew Jason and certain brethren to the rulers of the city, crying, These that have turned the world upside down are come here also.

ACTS 17:6

I beseech you therefore, brethren, by the mercies of God, that you present your bodies a living sacrifice, holy, acceptable to God, which is your reasonable service. And be not conformed to this world: but be you transformed by the renewing of your mind, that you may prove what is that good, and acceptable, and perfect, will of God. ROMANS 12:1–2

For who has known the mind of the Lord, that he may instruct Him? But we have the mind of Christ. 1 CORINTHIANS 2:16

For it is God which works in you both to will and to do of His good pleasure. PHILIPPIANS 2:13

And the very God of peace sanctify you wholly; and I pray God your whole spirit and soul and body be preserved blameless to the coming of our Lord Jesus Christ. 1 THESSALONIANS 5:23

By faith Enoch was translated that he should not see death; and was not found, because God had translated him: for before his translation he had this testimony, that he pleased God. HEBREWS 11:5

INSIGHTS ON FAITH FROM SMITH WIGGLESWORTH

God wants us to understand that whatever it costs, whatever it means, we must have a personal incoming of this life of God, this Holy Spirit, this divine person.

﹏

I want you to think about what it really means to receive the Holy Spirit. We are born again *"not of corruptible seed but incorruptible, through the word of God"* (1 Pet. 1:23). The Word *"lives and abides forever"* (v. 23). We are born again by the incorruptible power of God. It is His plan for us. This divine power is beyond anything that the human mind can conceive. We must have a divine mind in order to understand divine things.

﹏

When the Holy Spirit comes, He clothes and anoints the Christ who is already within the believer, who will be just the same only so much different; the power of the Spirit of the life of Christ is now being manifested in a new way, for this is the plan of God. You should be filled with the matter of the Word, for that is the life.

LIVING HOLY

Who is like You, O Lord, among the gods? Who is like You, glorious in holiness, fearful in praises, doing wonders? You stretched out your right hand, the earth swallowed them. You in Your mercy have led forth the people which You have redeemed: You have guided them in Your strength to Your holy habitation.

EXODUS 15:11–13

Sanctify yourselves therefore, and be you holy: for I am the Lord your God. And you shall keep my statutes, and do them: I am the Lord which sanctify you.

LEVITICUS 20:7–8

And now, Israel, what does the Lord your God require of you, but to fear the Lord your God, to walk in all His ways, and to love Him, and to serve the Lord your God with all your heart and with all your soul.

DEUTERONOMY 10:12

But take diligent heed to do the commandment and the law, which Moses the servant of the Lord charged you, to love the Lord your God, and to walk in all His ways, and to keep His commandments, and to cling to Him, and to serve Him with all your heart and with all your soul.

JOSHUA 22:5

And Samuel said, Has the Lord as great delight in burnt offerings and sacrifices, as in obeying the voice of the Lord? Behold, to obey is better than sacrifice, and to hearken than the fat of rams.

1 Samuel 15:22

Give to the Lord, you kindreds of the people, give to the Lord glory and strength. Give to the Lord the glory due to His name: bring an offering, and come before Him: worship the Lord in the beauty of holiness.

1 Chronicles 16:28–29

And you, Solomon my son, know you the God of your father, and serve Him with a perfect heart and with a willing mind: for the Lord searches all hearts, and understands all the imaginations of the thoughts: if you seek Him, He will be found of you; but if you forsake Him, He will cast you off for ever. 1 Chronicles 28:9

O that you had hearkened to My commandments! Then had your peace been as a river, and your righteousness as the waves of the sea.

Isaiah 48:18

But this thing commanded I them, saying, Obey My voice, and I will be your God, and you shall be My people: and walk you in all the ways that I have commanded you, that it may be well to you.

Jeremiah 7:23

Thus will I magnify Myself, and sanctify Myself; and I will be known in the eyes of many nations, and they shall know that I am the Lord.   EZEKIEL 38:23

And has raised up a horn of salvation for us in the house of His servant David.   LUKE 1:69

That He would grant to us, that we being delivered out of the hand of our enemies might serve Him without fear, in holiness and righteousness before Him, all the days of our life.
                                                               LUKE 1:74–75

But now being made free from sin, and become servants to God, you have your fruit to holiness, and the end everlasting life.
                                                                ROMANS 6:22

But now we are delivered from the law, that being dead wherein we were held; that we should serve in newness of spirit, and not in the oldness of the letter.   ROMANS 7:6

INSIGHTS ON FAITH FROM SMITH WIGGLESWORTH

The Holy Spirit wants you to sweep through darkness. The Holy Spirit wants to fill you with truth. The Holy Spirit wants to stimulate you in liberty. The Holy Spirit wants you to rise higher and higher.

⌣

If we are filled with the Spirit, then, in the hard place where the test comes, like the three Hebrew children, Shadrach, Meshach, and Abednego, our testimony is, "*We have no need to answer you in this matter.…Our God whom we serve is able to deliver us from the burning fiery furnace, and He will deliver us*" (Dan. 3:16–17). You cannot give thanks under such circumstances unless you are filled with the Spirit.

⌣

I have seen people filled with the Holy Spirit who used to be absolutely helpless, and when the power of God took their bodies, they became like young men instead of old, withered people. This is the power of the Holy Spirit.

LIVING HOLY

But of Him are you in Christ Jesus, who of God is made to us wisdom, and righteousness, and sanctification, and redemption.
1 CORINTHIANS 1:30

And what agreement has the temple of God with idols? For you are the temple of the living God; as God has said, I will dwell in them, and walk in them; and I will be their God, and they shall be My people.
2 CORINTHIANS 6:16

Having therefore these promises, dearly beloved, let us cleanse ourselves from all filthiness of the flesh and spirit, perfecting holiness in the fear of God.
2 CORINTHIANS 7:1

According as He has chosen us in Him before the foundation of the world, that we should be holy and without blame before Him in love.
EPHESIANS 1:4

Finally, brethren, whatsoever things are true, whatsoever things are honest, whatsoever things are just, whatsoever things are pure, whatsoever things are lovely, whatsoever things are of good report; if there be any virtue, and if there be any praise, think on these things.
PHILIPPIANS 4:8

To the end He may establish your hearts unblamable in holiness before God, even our Father, at the coming of our Lord Jesus Christ with all His saints. 1 THESSALONIANS 3:13

For God has not called us to uncleanness, but to holiness. 1 THESSALONIANS 4:7

And let ours also learn to maintain good works for necessary uses, that they be not unfruitful. TITUS 3:14

By the which will we are sanctified through the offering of the body of Jesus Christ once for all. HEBREWS 10:10

For they verily for a few days chastened us after their own pleasure; but He for our profit, that we might be partakers of His holiness. HEBREWS 12:10

Wherefore we receiving a kingdom which cannot be moved, let us have grace, whereby we may serve God acceptably with reverence and godly fear: for our God is a consuming fire.
HEBREWS 12:28–29

But as He which has called you is holy, so be you holy in all manner of conversation; because it is written, Be you holy; for I am holy. 1 PETER 1:15–16

LIVING WITH GENTLENESS

You have also given me the shield of Your salvation: and Your gentleness has made me great.   2 SAMUEL 22:36

You have also given me the shield of Your salvation: and Your right hand has held me up, and Your gentleness has made me great.   PSALM 18:35

A soft answer turns away wrath: but grievous words stir up anger.   PROVERBS 15:1

A wholesome tongue is a tree of life: but perverseness therein is a breach in the spirit.   PROVERBS 15:4

He shall feed his flock like a shepherd: He shall gather the lambs with His arm, and carry them in His bosom, and shall gently lead those that are with young.   ISAIAH 40:11

Blessed are the meek: for they shall inherit the earth.   MATTHEW 5:5

Or else how can one enter into a strong man's house, and spoil his goods, except he first bind the strong man? And then he will spoil his house.   MATTHEW 12:29

INSIGHTS ON FAITH FROM SMITH WIGGLESWORTH

Some people get a wrong idea of the baptism. The baptism is nothing less than the third person of the blessed Trinity coming down from the glory, the Spirit of the triune God—who carries out the will of the Father and the Son—dwelling in your body, revealing the truth to you, and causing you sometimes to say "Ah!" until your heart yearns with compassion, as Jesus yearned, so that you travail as He travailed, mourn as He mourned, groan as He groaned. It cannot be otherwise with you. You cannot get this thing in a merely passive way. It does not come that way. But, glory to God, it does come.

It is no little thing to be baptized with the Spirit; it is *"the Promise of the Father"* (v. 4). Jesus must be there, and the Holy Spirit also, bringing us to the place where we can be baptized. Are you going to treat it as a great thing? What do you really believe it is? I believe that when the Holy Spirit comes, He comes to crown the King. And from that day, the King gets His rightful place, and we don't have to claim anything; He becomes King of all situations.

LIVING WITH GENTLENESS

Now I Paul myself beseech you by the meekness and gentleness of Christ, who in presence am base among you, but being absent am bold toward you.   2 CORINTHIANS 10:1

Brethren, if a man be overtaken in a fault, you which are spiritual, restore such a one in the spirit of meekness; considering yourself, lest you also be tempted.   GALATIANS 6:1

If we live in the Spirit, let us also walk in the Spirit.
GALATIANS 5:25

For by grace are you saved through faith; and that not of yourselves: it is the gift of God: not of works, lest any man should boast.   EPHESIANS 2:8–9

With all lowliness and meekness, with longsuffering, forbearing one another in love.   EPHESIANS 4:2

Let your moderation be known to all men. The Lord is at hand.
PHILIPPIANS 4:5

And the Lord make you to increase and abound in love one toward another, and toward all men, even as we do toward you.
1 THESSALONIANS 3:12

But you, O man of God, flee these things; and follow after righteousness, godliness, faith, love, patience, meekness.

1 TIMOTHY 6:11

To speak evil of no man, to be no brawlers, but gentle, showing all meekness to all men. TITUS 3:2

Wherefore, my beloved brethren, let every man be swift to hear, slow to speak, slow to wrath: for the wrath of man works not the righteousness of God. JAMES 1:19–20

So speak you, and so do, as they that shall be judged by the law of liberty. For he shall have judgment without mercy, that has showed no mercy; and mercy rejoices against judgment.

JAMES 2:12–13

But the wisdom that is from above is first pure, then peaceable, gentle, and easy to be entreated, full of mercy and good fruits, without partiality, and without hypocrisy. JAMES 3:17

But sanctify the Lord God in your hearts: and be ready always to give an answer to every man that asks you a reason of the hope that is in you with meekness and fear. 1 PETER 3:15

LIVING WITH GRACE

For if you turn again to the Lord, your brethren and your children shall find compassion before them that lead them captive, so that they shall come again into this land: for the Lord your God is gracious and merciful, and will not turn away His face from you, if you return to Him.　　　　2 CHRONICLES 30:9

For God sent not His Son into the world to condemn the world; but that the world through Him might be saved.　　　JOHN 3:17

Verily, verily, I say to you, He that hears My word, and believes on Him that sent Me, has everlasting life, and shall not come into condemnation; but is passed from death to life.　　　JOHN 5:24

God forbid: yea, let God be true, but every man a liar; as it is written, that You might be justified in Your sayings, and might overcome when You are judged.　　　ROMANS 3:4

Therefore it is of faith, that it might be by grace; to the end the promise might be sure to all the seed; not to that only which is of the law, but to that also which is of the faith of Abraham; who is the father of us all.　　　ROMANS 4:16

INSIGHTS ON FAITH FROM SMITH WIGGLESWORTH

When I come into the presence of God, He takes the things of the Spirit and reveals them to me. Our hearts are comforted and built up. And there is no way to warm a heart more than by the heart that first touched the flame. There must be the heavenly fires burning within.

∽

Oh, the blessedness of being brought into a life of dependence upon the power of the Holy Spirit. Henceforth, we know that we are nothing without Him; we are absolutely dependent upon Him. I am absolutely nothing without the power and anointing of the Holy Spirit. Oh, for a life of absolute dependence! It is through a life of dependence that there is a life of power. If you are not there, get alone with God.

LIVING WITH GRACE

For sin shall not have dominion over you: for you are not under the law, but under grace. ROMANS 6:14

And if by grace, then is it no more of works: otherwise grace is no more grace. But if it be of works, then it is no more grace: otherwise work is no more work. ROMANS 11:6

But by the grace of God I am what I am: and His grace which was bestowed upon me was not in vain; but I labored more abundantly than they all: yet not I, but the grace of God which was with me. 1 CORINTHIANS 15:10

And God is able to make all grace abound toward you; that you, always having all sufficiency in all things, may abound to every good work. 2 CORINTHIANS 9:8

And He said to me, My grace is sufficient for you: for My strength is made perfect in weakness. Most gladly therefore will I rather glory in my infirmities, that the power of Christ may rest upon me. 2 CORINTHIANS 12:9

But God, who is rich in mercy, for His great love wherewith He loved us, even when we were dead in sins, has quickened us together with Christ, by grace you are saved. EPHESIANS 2:4–5

For by grace are you saved through faith; and that not of your-selves: it is the gift of God: not of works, lest any man should boast. Ephesians 2:8–9

Being filled with the fruits of righteousness, which are by Jesus Christ, to the glory and praise of God. Philippians 1:11

Which is come to you, as it is in all the world; and brings forth fruit, as it does also in you, since the day you heard of it, and knew the grace of God in truth. Colossians 1:6

But after that the kindness and love of God our Savior toward man appeared, not by works of righteousness which we have done, but according to His mercy He saved us, by the washing of regen-eration, and renewing of the Holy Ghost; which He shed on us abundantly through Jesus Christ our Savior; that being justified by His grace, we should be made heirs according to the hope of eternal life. Titus 3:4–7

For we have not an high priest which cannot be touched with the feeling of our infirmities; but was in all points tempted like as we are, yet without sin. Let us therefore come boldly to the throne of grace, that we may obtain mercy, and find grace to help in time of need. Hebrews 4:15–16

Looking diligently lest any man fail of the grace of God; lest any root of bitterness springing up trouble you, and thereby many be defiled. Hebrews 12:15

But He gives more grace. Wherefore He says, God resists the proud, but gives grace to the humble. JAMES 4:6

Grace and peace be multiplied to you through the knowledge of God, and of Jesus our Lord, according as His divine power has given to us all things that pertain to life and godliness, through the knowledge of Him that has called us to glory and virtue. 2 PETER 1:2–3

But grow in grace, and in the knowledge of our Lord and Savior Jesus Christ. To Him be glory both now and for ever. Amen. 2 PETER 3:18

Herein is love, not that we loved God, but that He loved us, and sent His Son to be the propitiation for our sins. 1 JOHN 4:10

Grace be with you, mercy, and peace, from God the Father, and from the Lord Jesus Christ, the Son of the Father, in truth and love. 2 JOHN 1:3

INSIGHTS ON FAITH FROM SMITH WIGGLESWORTH

Only by the Spirit can we understand what is spiritual. We cannot understand it on our own. We have to be spiritual to understand it. No man can understand the Word of God without his being quickened by the new nature. The Word of God is for the new nature. The Word of God is for the new life, to quicken mortal flesh.

❧

Do not forget that the Holy Spirit did not come as a cleanser. The Holy Spirit is not a cleanser; the Holy Spirit is a revealer of imperfection that can only be cleansed by the blood of Jesus. After the blood has cleansed you, you need the Word of God, for the Word of God is the only power that creates anew. Life comes through the Word. The Word is the Son; the Word is the life of the Son. He who has received the Son has received life; he who has not received the Son has not received life (John 3:36).

"HAVE GOD'S MIND ON THIS: GOD SAYS YOU HAVE TO OVERCOME THE WORLD, THAT YOU HAVE TO HAVE THIS INCORRUPTIBLE, UNDEFILED POSITION NOW WITHIN THE HUMAN BODY, TRANSFORMING YOUR MIND, EVEN YOUR VERY NATURE, REALIZING THE SUPERNATURAL POWER WORKING THROUGH YOU."

—SMITH WIGGLESWORTH

7

A SPIRIT-LED LIFE

ASSURANCE

For I am persuaded, that neither death, nor life, nor angels, nor principalities, nor powers, nor things present, nor things to come, nor height, nor depth, nor any other creature, shall be able to separate us from the love of God, which is in Christ Jesus our Lord.
ROMANS 8:38–39

For the which cause I also suffer these things: nevertheless I am not ashamed: for I know whom I have believed, and am persuaded that He is able to keep that which I have committed to him against that day.
2 TIMOTHY 1:12

And hereby we know that we are of the truth, and shall assure our hearts before Him.
1 JOHN 3:19

He that has the Son has life; and he that has not the Son of God has not life. These things have I written to you that believe on the name of the Son of God; that you may know that you have eternal life, and that you may believe on the name of the Son of God.
1 JOHN 5:12–13

BATTLE FOR YOUR MIND

Pride goes before destruction, and a haughty spirit before a fall.

PROVERBS 16:18

The spirit of man is the candle of the LORD, searching all the inward parts of the belly.   PROVERBS 20:27

And Jesus answered and said to them, Take heed that no man deceive you.   MATTHEW 24:4

And He said to them, Take heed what you hear: with what measure you mete, it shall be measured to you: and to you that hear shall more be given.   MARK 4:24

The Spirit of the Lord is upon Me, because He has anointed Me to preach the gospel to the poor; He has sent me to heal the brokenhearted, to preach deliverance to the captives, and recovering of sight to the blind, to set at liberty them that are bruised.

LUKE 4:18

Then said Jesus to those Jews which believed on Him, If you continue in My word, then are you My disciples indeed; and you shall know the truth, and the truth shall make you free.

JOHN 8:31–32

You are of your father the devil, and the lusts of your father you will do. He was a murderer from the beginning, and abode not in the truth, because there is no truth in him. When he speaks a lie, he speaks of his own: for he is a liar, and the father of it.

JOHN 8:44

For the weapons of our warfare are not carnal, but mighty through God to the pulling down of strong holds. Casting down imaginations, and every high thing that exalts itself against the knowledge of God, and bringing into captivity every thought to the obedience of Christ.

2 CORINTHIANS 10:4–5

This I say therefore, and testify in the Lord, that you hereafter walk not as other Gentiles walk, in the vanity of their mind.

EPHESIANS 4:17

Be careful for nothing; but in every thing by prayer and supplication with thanksgiving let your requests be made known to God. And the peace of God, which passes all understanding, shall keep your hearts and minds through Christ Jesus. Finally, brethren, whatsoever things are true, whatsoever things are honest, whatsoever things are just, whatsoever things are pure, whatsoever things are lovely, whatsoever things are of good report; if there be any virtue, and if there be any praise, think on these things.

PHILIPPIANS 4:6–8

INSIGHTS ON FAITH FROM SMITH WIGGLESWORTH

God's command is for us to *"be filled with the Spirit"* (Eph. 5:18). We are no good if we have only a full cup. We need to have an overflowing cup all the time. It is a tragedy not to live in the fullness of overflowing. See that you never live below the overflowing tide.

～

May God take us on and on into this glorious fact of faith, so that we may be so in the Holy Spirit that God will work through us along the lines of the miraculous and along the lines of prophecy. When we are operating in the Spirit, we will always know that it is no longer we but He who is working through us, bringing forth what is in His own divine good pleasure (Phil. 2:13).

～

As you yield to the Spirit of the Lord, He has power over your intellect, over your heart, and over your voice. The Holy Spirit has power to unveil Christ and to project the vision of Christ upon the canvas of your mind. Then He uses your tongue to glorify and magnify Him in a way that you could never do apart from the Spirit's power.

BATTLE FOR YOUR MIND

Who has delivered us from the power of darkness, and has translated us into the kingdom of His dear Son.   COLOSSIANS 1:13

Let no man beguile you of your reward in a voluntary humility and worshipping of angels, intruding into those things which he has not seen, vainly puffed up by his fleshly mind.
COLOSSIANS 2:18

Let no man deceive you by any means: for that day shall not come, except there come a falling away first, and that man of sin be revealed, the son of perdition.   2 THESSALONIANS 2:3

Who are kept by the power of God through faith to salvation ready to be revealed in the last time.   1 PETER 1:5

But there were false prophets also among the people, even as there shall be false teachers among you, who secretly shall bring in damnable heresies, even denying the Lord that bought them, and bring upon themselves swift destruction.   2 PETER 2:1

Little children, let no man deceive you: he that does righteousness is righteous, even as He is righteous.   1 JOHN 3:7

BOLDNESS

Behold, I send you forth as sheep in the midst of wolves: be you therefore wise as serpents, and harmless as doves.

MATTHEW 10:16

The Spirit itself bears witness with our spirit, that we are the children of God: and if children, then heirs; heirs of God, and joint-heirs with Christ; if so be that we suffer with Him, that we may be also glorified together. ROMANS 8:16–17

Now thanks be to God, which always causes us to triumph in Christ, and makes manifest the savor of His knowledge by us in every place. 2 CORINTHIANS 2:14

And such trust have we through Christ to toward God: not that we are sufficient of ourselves to think any thing as of ourselves; but our sufficiency is of God. 2 CORINTHIANS 3:4–5

For God, who commanded the light to shine out of darkness, has shined in our hearts, to give the light of the knowledge of the glory of God in the face of Jesus Christ. 2 CORINTHIANS 4:6

BREAKTHROUGHS

Surely He shall deliver you from the snare of the fowler, and from the noisome pestilence. He shall cover you with His feathers, and under His wings shall you trust: His truth shall be your shield and buckler. You shall not be afraid for the terror by night; nor for the arrow that flies by day.   PSALM 91:3–5

The LORD your God in the midst of you is mighty; He will save, He will rejoice over you with joy; He will rest in His love, He will joy over you with singing. I will gather them that are sorrowful for the solemn assembly, who are of you, to whom the reproach of it was a burden. Behold, at that time I will undo all that afflict you: and I will save her that halts, and gather her that was driven out; and I will get them praise and fame in every land where they have been put to shame. At that time will I bring you again, even in the time that I gather you: for I will make you a name and a praise among all people of the earth, when I turn back your captivity before your eyes, says the LORD.   ZEPHANIAH 3:17–20

To the intent that now to the principalities and powers in heavenly places might be known by the church the manifold wisdom of God.   EPHESIANS 3:10

INSIGHTS ON FAITH FROM SMITH WIGGLESWORTH

As we are filled with the Holy Spirit, our one desire is to glorify Him. We need to be filled with the Spirit to get the full revelation of the Lord Jesus Christ.

∽

In Romans 8:27, we read, *"He who searches the hearts knows what the mind of the Spirit is, because He makes intercession for the saints according to the will of God."* Many times, as we speak to God in an unknown tongue, we are in intercession; and as we pray thus in the Spirit, we pray according to the will of God. And there is such a thing as the Spirit making intercession *"with groanings which cannot be uttered"* (v. 26).

∽

Beloved, if there is anything in your life that in any way resists the power of the Holy Spirit and the entrance of His Word into your heart and life, drop on your knees and cry aloud for mercy. When the Spirit of God is waiting at your heart's door, do not resist Him; instead, open your heart to the touch of God.

CONFORMING TO THE SPIRIT

And you shall know that I am the LORD: for you have not walked in My statutes, neither executed My judgments, but have done after the manners of the heathen that are round about you.

EZEKIEL 11:12

Blessed are the peacemakers: for they shall be called the children of God.　　　　　　　　　　　　　　　　　　MATTHEW 5:9

Let us therefore follow after the things which make for peace, and things wherewith one may edify another.　　　ROMANS 14:19

Be you not unequally yoked together with unbelievers: for what fellowship has righteousness with unrighteousness? And what communion has light with darkness?　　2 CORINTHIANS 6:14

Wherefore come out from among them, and be you separate, says the Lord, and touch not the unclean thing; and I will receive you. And will be a Father to you, and you shall be my sons and daughters, says the Lord Almighty.　　　2 CORINTHIANS 6:17–18

As obedient children, not fashioning yourselves according to the former lusts in your ignorance: but as He which has called you is holy, so be you holy in all manner of conversation.

1 PETER 1:14–15

CRY OF THE SPIRIT

For he shall be great in the sight of the Lord, and shall drink neither wine nor strong drink; and he shall be filled with the Holy Ghost, even from his mother's womb. LUKE 1:15

Annas and Caiaphas being the high priests, the word of God came to John the son of Zacharias in the wilderness. And he came into all the country about Jordan, preaching the baptism of repentance for the remission of sins. LUKE 3:2–3

Every valley shall be filled, and every mountain and hill shall be brought low; and the crooked shall be made straight, and the rough ways shall be made smooth; and all flesh shall see the salvation of God. LUKE 3:5–6

And this is the record of John, when the Jews sent priests and Levites from Jerusalem to ask him, Who are you? And he confessed, and denied not; but confessed, I am not the Christ. And they asked him, What then? Are you Elijah? And he says, I am not. Are you that prophet? And he answered, No.... He said, I am the voice of one crying in the wilderness, make straight the way of the Lord, as said the prophet Isaiah. JOHN 1:19–21, 23

And John bore record, saying, I saw the Spirit descending from heaven like a dove, and It abode upon Him. And I knew Him not: but He that sent me to baptize with water, the same said to me, Upon whom you shall see the Spirit descending, and remaining on Him, the same is He which baptizes with the Holy Ghost. And I saw, and bore record that this is the Son of God.

JOHN 1:32–34

Then Peter said to them, Repent, and be baptized every one of you in the name of Jesus Christ for the remission of sins, and you shall receive the gift of the Holy Ghost.

ACTS 2:38

And make straight paths for your feet, lest that which is lame be turned out of the way; but let it rather be healed.

HEBREWS 12:13

But the anointing which you have received of Him abides in you, and you need not that any man teach you: but as the same anointing teaches you of all things, and is truth, and is no lie, and even as it has taught you, you shall abide in Him.

1 JOHN 2:27

INSIGHTS ON FAITH FROM SMITH WIGGLESWORTH

Before the Holy Spirit can have His way within you, you must be cleansed from your own evil appetites; there must be a body prepared for the Holy Spirit.

⸺

The baptism of the Holy Spirit is necessary, for then the Holy Spirit will so reveal the Word in the body that it will be like a sword; it will cut between the soul and the spirit; it will cut it right out until the soulishness cannot long to indulge in things contrary to the mind of God and the will of God anymore. Don't you want rest? How long are you going to wait before you enter into that rest? *"There remains therefore a rest for the people of God"* (Heb. 4:9). God wants you to enter into that rest.

⸺

So the Holy Spirit is to make us ready for every perfect work, ready in such a way that opportunities are taken advantage of. Just as much as if the Lord Jesus were in the world, we must be in the world, ready for the glorious, blessed anointing and equipping for service. In this way, the powers of hell will not prevail (Matt. 16:18); we will bind the powers of Satan. We will be in a great position to engage in spiritual battle.

GIFTS FROM THE SPIRIT

I indeed baptize you with water to repentance. but He that comes after me is mightier than I, whose shoes I am not worthy to bear: He shall baptize you with the Holy Ghost, and with fire.

MATTHEW 3:11

While Peter yet spoke these words, the Holy Ghost fell on all them which heard the word. And they of the circumcision which believed were astonished, as many as came with Peter, because that on the Gentiles also was poured out the gift of the Holy Ghost. For they heard them speak with tongues, and magnify God.

ACTS 10:44–46

Having then gifts differing according to the grace that is given to us, whether prophecy, let us prophesy according to the proportion of faith.

ROMANS 12:6

Now there are diversities of gifts, but the same Spirit…. And there are diversities of operations, but it is the same God which works all in all. But the manifestation of the Spirit is given to every man to profit withal.

1 CORINTHIANS 12:4, 6–7

Even so you, forasmuch as you are zealous of spiritual gifts, seek that you may excel to the edifying of the church.

1 CORINTHIANS 14:12

I thank my God, I speak with tongues more than you all: yet in the church I had rather speak five words with my understanding, that by my voice I might teach others also, than ten thousand words in an unknown tongue.   1 CORINTHIANS 14:18–19

And He gave some, apostles; and some, prophets; and some, evangelists; and some, pastors and teachers; for the perfecting of the saints, for the work of the ministry, for the edifying of the body of Christ.   EPHESIANS 4:11–12

Neglect not the gift that is in you, which was given you by prophecy, with the laying on of the hands of the presbytery. Meditate upon these things; give yourself wholly to them; that your profiting may appear to all.   1 TIMOTHY 4:14–15

As every man has received the gift, even so minister the same one to another, as good stewards of the manifold grace of God. If any man speak, let him speak as the oracles of God; if any man minister, let him do it as of the ability which God gives: that God in all things may be glorified through Jesus Christ, to whom be praise and dominion for ever and ever. Amen.   1 PETER 4:10–11

OUR INHERITANCE

Therefore my heart is glad, and my glory rejoices: my flesh also shall rest in hope.　　　　　　　　　　　　　　PSALM 16:9

One thing have I desired of the LORD, that will I seek after; that I may dwell in the house of the LORD all the days of my life, to behold the beauty of the LORD, and to enquire in His temple.

PSALM 27:4

The sacrifices of God are a broken spirit: a broken and a contrite heart, O God, You will not despise.　　　　　　PSALM 51:17

Verily, verily, I say to you, we speak that we do know, and testify that we have seen; and you receive not our witness. If I have told you earthly things, and you believe not, how shall you believe, if I tell you of heavenly things? And no man has ascended up to heaven, but He that came down from heaven, even the Son of man which is in heaven.　　　　　　　　　　JOHN 3:11–13

And now, brethren, I commend you to God, and to the word of His grace, which is able to build you up, and to give you an inheritance among all them which are sanctified.　　　ACTS 20:32

INSIGHTS ON FAITH FROM SMITH WIGGLESWORTH

To me, the baptism of the Holy Spirit is not a goal; it is an infilling that allows us to reach the highest level, the holiest position that it is possible for human nature to reach. The baptism of the Holy Spirit comes to reveal Him who is filled fully with God. So I see that to be baptized with the Holy Spirit is to be baptized into death, into life, into power, into fellowship with the Trinity, where we cease to be and God takes us forever.

In the baptism of the Holy Spirit, there is unlimited grace and endurance as the Spirit reveals Himself to us. The excellency of Christ can never be understood apart from illumination. And I find that the Holy Spirit is the great Illuminator who makes me understand all the depths of Him.

The Holy Spirit is the great Motivator of us all. He receives all, He disburses all, and He sends out the wonderful manifestations after He has had the call. So we must have life in the Spirit, united, illuminated, transformed all the time by this glorious regenerating power of the Spirit. May God reveal that it is for us all.

OUR INHERITANCE

For we know that if our earthly house of this tabernacle were dissolved, we have a building of God, a house not made with hands, eternal in the heavens.　　　　　2 CORINTHIANS 5:1

Wherefore you are no more a servant, but a son; and if a son, then an heir of God through Christ.　　　　　GALATIANS 4:7

Blessed be the God and Father of our Lord Jesus Christ, who has blessed us with all spiritual blessings in heavenly places in Christ.　　　　　EPHESIANS 1:3

The eyes of your understanding being enlightened; that you may know what is the hope of His calling, and what the riches of the glory of His inheritance in the saints.　　　　　EPHESIANS 1:18

Whereof I was made a minister, according to the gift of the grace of God given to me by the effectual working of His power.
　　　　　EPHESIANS 3:7

Being born again, not of corruptible seed, but of incorruptible, by the word of God, which lives and abides for ever.　　1 PETER 1:23

SPEAKING TO MOUNTAINS

The mountains melted from before the LORD, *even that Sinai from before the* LORD *God of Israel.*   JUDGES 5:5

He puts forth His hand upon the rock; He overturns the mountains by the roots.   JOB 28:9

I will make waste mountains and hills, and dry up all their herbs; and I will make the rivers islands, and I will dry up the pools.   ISAIAH 42:15

The mountains saw You, and they trembled: the overflowing of the water passed by: the deep uttered his voice, and lifted up his hands on high.   HABAKKUK 3:10

For verily I say to you, That whosoever shall say to this mountain, Be you removed, and be you cast into the sea; and shall not doubt in his heart, but shall believe that those things which he says shall come to pass; he shall have whatsoever he says.   MARK 11:23

INSIGHTS ON FAITH FROM SMITH WIGGLESWORTH

But as you live in the Spirit, you move, act, eat, drink, and do everything to the glory of God (1 Cor. 10:31). Our message is always this: "Be filled with the Spirit." This is God's place for you, and it is as far above the natural life as the heavens are above the earth. Yield yourself so that God will fill you.

God does not want us to fall but to be kept by His grace from falling, and He wants us to strive for holiness. I see the Word of God is the living Word, and Jesus is the Author of the Word. The Holy Spirit is the enlightener of the Word. If you look at Acts 1, you will see these words: *"He through the Holy Spirit had given commandments."*

I want you to have an inward knowledge that there is a power in you that is greater than any other power. And I trust that, by the help of the Spirit, I may bring you into a place of deliverance, a place of holy sanctification where you dare to stand against the *"wiles of the devil"* (Eph. 6:11), drive them back, and cast them out.

THE SPIRIT OF THE LORD IS UPON ME

Trust in the LORD *with all your heart; and lean not to your own understanding. In all your ways acknowledge Him, and He shall direct your paths. Be not wise in your own eyes: fear the* LORD, *and depart from evil.*　　　　　　　　　　　　PROVERBS 3:5–7

So shall My word be that goes forth out of My mouth: it shall not return to Me void, but it shall accomplish that which I please, and it shall prosper in the thing whereto I sent it.　　ISAIAH 55:11

And I will give to you the keys of the kingdom of heaven: and whatsoever you shall bind on earth shall be bound in heaven: and whatsoever you shall loose on earth shall be loosed in heaven.

MATTHEW 16:19

The Spirit of the Lord is upon me, because He has anointed me to preach the gospel to the poor; He has sent me to heal the brokenhearted, to preach deliverance to the captives, and recovering of sight to the blind, to set at liberty them that are bruised, to preach the acceptable year of the Lord.　　　　　　LUKE 4:18–19

And He said, The things which are impossible with men are possible with God.　　　　　　　　　　　　　　LUKE 18:27

But the Comforter, which is the Holy Ghost, whom the Father will send in My name, He shall teach you all things, and bring all things to your remembrance, whatsoever I have said to you.

JOHN 14:26

And hope makes not ashamed; because the love of God is shed abroad in our hearts by the Holy Ghost which is given to us.

ROMANS 5:5

And God has set some in the church, first apostles, secondarily prophets, thirdly teachers, after that miracles, then gifts of healings, helps, governments, diversities of tongues.

1 CORINTHIANS 12:28

Knowing this first, that no prophecy of the scripture is of any private interpretation.

2 PETER 1:20

Love not the world, neither the things that are in the world. If any man love the world, the love of the Father is not in him. For all that is in the world, the lust of the flesh, and the lust of the eyes, and the pride of life, is not of the Father, but is of the world. And the world passes away, and the lust thereof: but he that does the will of God abides for ever.

1 JOHN 2:15–17

TEACHING OF THE HOLY SPIRIT

The spirit of God has made me, and the breath of the Almighty has given me life.   JOB 33:4

Jesus answered, Verily, verily, I say to you, Except a man be born of water and of the Spirit, he cannot enter into the kingdom of God.   JOHN 3:5

Even the Spirit of truth; whom the world cannot receive, because it sees Him not, neither knows Him: but you know Him; for He dwells with you, and shall be in you.   JOHN 14:17

But the Comforter, which is the Holy Ghost, whom the Father will send in My name, He shall teach you all things, and bring all things to your remembrance, whatsoever I have said to you.   JOHN 14:26

But when the Comforter is come, whom I will send to you from the Father, even the Spirit of truth, which proceeds from the Father, He shall testify of Me.   JOHN 15:26

However when He, the Spirit of truth, is come, He will guide you into all truth: for He shall not speak of Himself; but whatsoever He shall hear, that shall He speak: and He will show you things to come.   JOHN 16:13

And the angel answered and said to her, The Holy Ghost shall come upon you, and the power of the Highest shall overshadow you: therefore also that holy thing which shall be born of you shall be called the Son of God. **LUKE 1:35**

The Spirit itself bears witness with our spirit, that we are the children of God. **ROMANS 8:16**

But God has revealed them to us by His Spirit: for the Spirit searches all things, yea, the deep things of God.

1 CORINTHIANS 2:10

In whom you also trusted, after that you heard the word of truth, the gospel of your salvation: in whom also after that you believed, you were sealed with that holy Spirit of promise.

EPHESIANS 1:13

And grieve not the Holy Spirit of God, whereby you are sealed to the day of redemption. **EPHESIANS 4:30**

Not by works of righteousness which we have done, but according to His mercy He saved us, by the washing of regeneration, and renewing of the Holy Ghost. **TITUS 3:5**

INSIGHTS ON FAITH FROM SMITH WIGGLESWORTH

Jesus, our Mediator and Advocate, was filled with the Holy Spirit. He commanded His followers concerning these days we are in and gave instructions about the time through the Holy Spirit. I can see that if we are going to accomplish anything, we are going to accomplish it because we are under the power of the Holy Spirit.

~

Beloved, if you come into perfect line with the grace of God, one thing will certainly take place in your life. You will change from that old position of the world where you are judging everybody and not trusting anybody, and you will come into a place where you will have a heart that will believe all things, a heart that under no circumstances retaliates when you are insulted.

~

The Holy Spirit wants everybody to see the unveiling of Jesus. The unveiling of Jesus is to take away yourself and to place Him in you, to take away all your human weakness and put within you that wonderful Word of eternal power and of eternal life that makes you believe that all things are possible.

YOU'VE RECEIVED, NOW BELIEVE

My son, forget not my law; but let your heart keep my command-ments: for length of days, and long life, and peace, shall they add to you. PROVERBS 3:1–2

Blessed are the pure in heart: for they shall see God.
MATTHEW 5:8

Go you therefore, and teach all nations, baptizing them in the name of the Father, and of the Son, and of the Holy Ghost.
MATTHEW 28:19

And these signs shall follow them that believe; in My name shall they cast out devils; they shall speak with new tongues.
MARK 16:17

In Him was life; and the life was the light of men. JOHN 1:4

Hereafter I will not talk much with you: for the prince of this world comes, and has nothing in Me. JOHN 14:30

By whom also we have access by faith into this grace wherein we stand, and rejoice in hope of the glory of God. ROMANS 5:2

For the law of the Spirit of life in Christ Jesus has made me free from the law of sin and death. ROMANS 8:2

But when we are judged, we are chastened of the Lord, that we should not be condemned with the world.

1 CORINTHIANS 11:32

For we that are in this tabernacle do groan, being burdened: not for that we would be unclothed, but clothed upon, that mortality might be swallowed up of life. 2 CORINTHIANS 5:4

Set your affection on things above, not on things on the earth.

COLOSSIANS 3:2

Lie not one to another, seeing that you have put off the old man with his deeds; and have put on the new man, which is renewed in knowledge after the image of Him that created him.

COLOSSIANS 3:9–10

And let the peace of God rule in your hearts, to the which also you are called in one body; and be you thankful.

COLOSSIANS 3:15

And whatsoever you do in word or deed, do all in the name of the Lord Jesus, giving thanks to God and the Father by Him.

COLOSSIANS 3:17

But after that the kindness and love of God our Savior toward man appeared, not by works of righteousness which we have done, but according to His mercy He saved us, by the washing of regeneration, and renewing of the Holy Ghost; which He shed on us abundantly through Jesus Christ our Savior; that being justified by His grace, we should be made heirs according to the hope of eternal life. TITUS 3:4–7

But whoso looks into the perfect law of liberty, and continues therein, he being not a forgetful hearer, but a doer of the work, this man shall be blessed in his deed. JAMES 1:25

Forasmuch then as Christ has suffered for us in the flesh, arm yourselves likewise with the same mind: for he that has suffered in the flesh has ceased from sin; that he no longer should live the rest of his time in the flesh to the lusts of men, but to the will of God. 1 PETER 4:1–2

He that loves his brother abides in the light, and there is no occasion of stumbling in him. But he that hates his brother is in darkness, and walks in darkness, and knows not where he goes, because that darkness has blinded his eyes. 1 JOHN 2:10–11

"HALLELUJAH! THE SPIRIT BREATHES, THE SPIRIT LIFTS, THE SPIRIT RENEWS, THE SPIRIT QUICKENS. HE BRINGS LIFE WHERE DEATH WAS. HE BRINGS TRUTH WHERE NO VISION WAS. HE BRINGS REVELATION, FOR GOD IS IN THAT MAN. HE IS IN THE POWER OF THE SPIRIT, LOST, HIDDEN, CLOTHED, FILLED, AND RESURRECTED."

—SMITH WIGGLESWORTH

MY FAVORITE BIBLE PROMISES

_____

_____

_____

_____

_____

_____

_____

_____

_____

_____

OTHER BOOKS IN THE GREATEST BIBLE PROMISE BOOK SERIES....

The Greatest Bible Promises for Healing and Comfort

There is comfort in knowing that the hardest things are just lifting places into the grace of God. He is our Deliverer. This collection of Scripture promises helps the reader understand that, in these times, God wants to bring us through our needs and into the victory He has for us. Wigglesworth's wisdom helps us learn to let go of our challenges and see God take hold and hold us up.

The Greatest Bible Promises for Faith and Miracles

The harder the place you are in, the more blessing can come out of it as you seek God's plan. These special Scripture verses with Wigglesworth's teaching provide the wisdom of God's plan in its fullness. Readers will discover faith-building truths that can lead to miracles in a life yielded to the blessings God eagerly wants to give us.

The Smith Wigglesworth quotes throughout this book were taken from the following Whitaker House published titles...

Smith Wigglesworth on Faith
978-0-88368-531-0

> Faith is a gift of God that is available to all who will receive it.

Smith Wigglesworth: The Power of Faith
978-0-88368-608-9

> The sustaining effect of the smallest drop of faith will create continual ripples of power.

Smith Wigglesworth on Ever Increasing Faith
978-0-88368-633-1

> Join the evangelist in the great adventure called "faith."

Smith Wigglesworth on the Power of Scripture
978-1-60374-094-4

> You will cherish this glimpse into the heart and mind of one of God's most gifted servants.

Smith Wigglesworth on the Anointing
978-0-88368-530-3

> As you live in His anointing, your spiritual life will become more fruitful.

Smith Wigglesworth on the Holy Spirit
978-0-88368-544-0

> Learn how the fullness of the Holy Spirit can be yours.

Smith Wigglesworth on Healing
978-0-88368-426-9

> Not only can you be healed of your sicknesses, but God can use you to bring healing to others.

Smith Wigglesworth on Spiritual Gifts
978-0-88368-533-4

> You can be the instrument God uses to transmit His love and miracles to others.

Smith Wigglesworth on Heaven
978-0-88368-954-7

> Discover God's plans for you in this life and what He has in store for you in the heaven.

The beloved, classic KJV text with its language updated to modern equivalents without any doctrinal changes.

W
WHITAKER
HOUSE

In this translation, the trusted KJV text remains doctrinally intact, but its archaic language and difficult words have been replaced for clarity with their modern equivalents.

This Bible is also a complete red letter edition, meaning that the direct words of God are indicated in red in both the Old and New Testaments—currently the only Bible with this feature.

If you want to pass along the KJV that you know and love to the next generation of believers without compromising the translation that you trust, the KJVER is the Bible for you.

The Trusted King James in an Easy Read Format ™

whitakerhouse.com/kjver

Hope

Hope

Wisdom to Survive in a Hopeless World

Devdutt Pattanaik

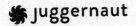

JUGGERNAUT BOOKS
C-I-128, First Floor, Sangam Vihar,
Near Holi Chowk, New Delhi 110080, India

First published by Juggernaut Books 2021

10 9 8 7 6 5 4 3 2

P-ISBN: 9789391165529
E-ISBN: 9789391165567

Typeset in Adobe Caslon Pro by
R. Ajith Kumar, Noida

Printed at Thomson Press India Ltd

Contents

Introduction

Wasn't the world supposed to be a better place in the twenty-first century? But the world we live in feels bleaker than ever. There is climate change, social inequality, mental stress, and the relentless fight on social media on trivial matters between sensible people who insist they are right. We have so many tools to communicate yet feel more disconnected than ever. The COVID-19 crisis has only amplified the sense of hopelessness in many. How can we be resilient and find positivity? How can we develop our mental and emotional strength to live joyfully?

In this book, I want to enable you to hope again by looking at the world with fresh eyes. And I am going to do this through stories you may have heard as a child, but by lending new meanings.

Chapter 1 begins by acknowledging hopelessness as an emotion. Using the mythologies from around the world, I want to show you that despair and devastation have always been a part of the human experience.

Chapter 2 explores how tales of abundance inspire us and establish hope in our minds, even as they shield us from life's harsh realities.

Chapter 3 traces the origins of a crisis and triggers of hopelessness that impact our objective as well as subjective realities. Our mind can make things far worse.

Chapter 4 focuses on what we can do in a crisis, for ourselves and for others.

Chapter 5 takes a long-term view so that we can continue to be hopeful about a better tomorrow while being realistic and resilient enough to handle a crisis, should it come along.

The first three chapters explore ideas that may help you shift your way of thinking. The last two are more practical, giving you coping strategies to manage a crisis.

God is particularly capitalized in the book when referring to divinity in Judeo-Christian-Islamic contexts, as these faiths are monotheistic.

Introduction

In Hinduism, the divine spectrum can be God, Goddess, god, goddess. The words have myriad meanings depending on the context. They do not always refer to entities but to ideas located within and around us.

Think of this book as a house with many doors. You open the front door of a house and enter a dark room – the first chapter. The room leads to another. This too is dark but perhaps a little less so. The second opens into a third, which is relatively lighter. And so on. From darkness into light. But in that light you will find the strength to face darkness, should you encounter such a room once again.

This book does not claim to be The Truth. It presents coping skills that I have encountered in my reading of Indian and world mythologies over the past twenty-five years. Read them keeping in mind:

Within infinite myths lies an eternal truth
Who sees it all?
Varuna has but a thousand eyes
Indra, a hundred
You and I, only two

1

Feeling hopeless

'I feel hopeless. I spent days trying to find a hospital bed for my uncle. I finally managed to, but he couldn't make it. I failed to find one for my aunt until it was too late for her too. Then my father got sick. I tried everything I could, made all the phone calls, but I couldn't save him. The older generation in my family is gone – in a matter of weeks. I just don't know how to process this.'

'I have lost my job. I am the only person supporting my family. What will I do?'

'I am single, and my aged mother lives with me. I have a salary cut. I need to support myself and her. What is the way out?'

'What about my children? The schools have shut for over a year. What is going to happen to their future?'

'My five-year-old hasn't met a single friend this last year. I worry about the pollution too. What kind of a world are we raising them in?'

'The government is not here to support me in any way, and I'm feeling scared. The country seems so full of anger. So much violence. I don't see hope for this country. Should I emigrate if I can? But where will I go?'

'I lost my wife, who was pregnant with an eight-month-old child. Why did I have to lose her? What happened? She was healthy. I have to now look after our four-year-old boy all by myself. Can I do it? How can I go on?'

'I want to get out of this WhatsApp group, this Facebook group, this society where I reside, this office, this family . . . Everyone seems to be just fighting, arguing, being rude, and disrespectful. No one is listening to anyone. I need to breathe. Just be . . . maybe be with people who care. I just want to feel safe.'

Hopelessness emerges when we are convinced the world does not grant us opportunities, when we feel overwhelmed by challenges and threats, when we feel weak, stripped of all strength, with no helping hand around, no angel, no guardian, no saviour, no shepherd. When we feel abandoned by family, friends, state, and god.

People often blame the current widespread state of hopelessness on instant news and the access to social media. If social media did not exist, we wouldn't't have to hear of hospital queues, job losses, and stories of pain from strangers. We want to believe the world is better than the negativity that gets marketed, better than what it was in the past.

Yet the world's mythologies – the sacred stories of ancient cultures transmitted over generations – tell a different story. Many, indeed you could say most, myths are stories about hopelessness and crisis. This current state where the world feels apocalyptic is not unique. It has always been so. Let us take a look at these stories, from India and beyond, from different religions. In this chapter, we will:

- Explore India's oldest scriptures, the Vedas, and meet a boy called Sunahshepa who stands for hopelessness more deeply and poignantly than any character I know.

- Witness the struggle of Gajendra, the mighty king of elephants, in a lotus pond, in Buddhist and Hindu art.
- Learn how prophets and messengers (paigambars) of Abrahamic religions (Judaism, Christianity, and Islam) spoke of hope amid utter despair.
- Read stories of crises from our great epics, the Ramayana and the Mahabharata.
- Look at how death has rendered even gods-on-earth (avatars) helpless but not hopeless.

The purpose of this chapter is to make us realize that we are not alone in our misery. Despair and desperation are universal but not eternal.

Abandoned in the Vedas

Hinduism's most ancient texts, the Vedas tell the story of a young boy called Sunahshepa. The story begins with a king who is very ill. He invokes a god and offers to sacrifice his son if cured. The god cures the king, but the ruler now hesitates to offer his son. He consults his ministers, and they come up with a way out: adopt a son and sacrifice the adopted son. The king likes the idea. Proclamations are sent across the land. The king wants a son, messengers and heralds put out the word.

Everyone is excited. Who doesn't want their son to become a prince? But as soon as they hear what is to follow – the dark condition – they recoil in horror. Give up our son to be executed? No, never! After great difficulty, the king's men find one man who says he is willing to give up his son. When he presents himself at the palace, the king asks, 'Why are you giving your son away?' The man replies, 'I'm very poor and have no food to eat. And you are promising us a thousand cows. It will change our fortunes.'

The king is still dissatisfied. 'But you're giving up your son,' he says. 'Can you live with that?' The man says, 'I have three sons. The eldest son is dear to me, the youngest is dear to the mother. This one in the middle, we can spare.'

And so the boy, Sunahshepa, is taken to the sacrificial altar. But now arises another complication. The priests refuse to go ahead. They say, 'We cannot sacrifice a human being. We will sacrifice an animal, a plant, but a human, this cannot be done.' 'Why don't you do it?' they ask the king.

And the king says, 'I don't want to do it either.' He decides that he will give another thousand cows to anyone who sacrifices the boy. The boy's father returns and says he would be happy to do it. The king looks at the father in disbelief. 'The first time your excuse was poverty. What's your excuse this time,' he asks.

Sunahshepa is listening to this conversation. He thinks to himself in despair, 'I have been abandoned by my father. I've been abandoned by my king, and a god wants me as sacrifice. Where do I go? Who do I cry out to? Who will come to my rescue? The people who are supposed to take care of me – my family, the state, and even god – seem to be against me.' He feels hopeless.

What happened to Sunahshepa? The story goes that the gods finally intervened and saved his life. I have always found this story deeply powerful – the boy's utter helplessness and aloneness embody the emotions all of us feel in our time of darkness. Who is there for me? Will anyone help? What can I do?

Sunahshepa embodies the feeling of hopelessness of a child who when abandoned looks for the support of others, especially the almighty, to survive. Is that god within us? Are we to save Sunahshepa? Or are we Sunahshepa?

Elephantine struggles in Jatakas and Puranas

The Buddhist stupa at Barhut, Madhya Pradesh, built two thousand years ago, has an image depicting an incident from the Jataka stories, where a mighty elephant in a lotus pond enjoying himself in the water is grabbed by a crab that threatens to drown him. The bull elephant is being dragged under, and he cannot do anything about it. All the cow elephants who were with him have abandoned him because they are terrified of the crab, and they want to protect themselves. He's on his own. Utterly alone, feeling completely abandoned.

We find a very similar image in one of the earliest Hindu temples, the Dasavatara temple in Deogarh. Here you have a carving of an elephant being dragged down by not a crab but a Naga, one of the half-human, half-snake semi-divine creatures of Hindu myths. As before, he is bellowing in fear, raising his trunk, holding a lotus flower, begging for help. This tale of drowning is elaborated in the Bhagavata Purana. Here, the snake is replaced by a crocodile.

In Hindu art and literature, the elephant-king is rescued by the four-armed Vishnu, who descends from the sky on his vehicle Garuda, the eagle, and hurls a discus to kill the villain. In the Buddhist art, the elephant is later shown crushing the crab with his foot, with a little help from his chief queen whose wailing, the story goes, distracted the villain momentarily.

Both the Hindu and the Buddhist stories speak of a hopeless situation, in the lotus pond. The crab/snake/crocodile is the cause of hopelessness. The lotus pond is the world of abundance we desire.

Why has the crocodile, Naga or crab decided to grab you and destroy you? It wants to survive;

it has nothing against you. There is nothing personal. COVID-19 is not our enemy, nor is the economic downturn. It's just that we are part of this horrifying situation, standing right in the middle of it. And we are drowning.

The meaninglessness is a central part of our despair. Why were we chosen? If there was a reason – such as this man hates me and he's destroying me, or I have hurt this man and therefore he's hurting me back – it would have helped to understand better. But during the pandemic the questions that came to us were, why is a good person suffering? Why me? Do I deserve such a fate? Why me and not them?

In the Jataka tale, the elephant fights the battle himself and wins against the giant crab. In the Hindu stories, help arrives from outside, from Vishnu the protector. In one case, hopelessness is tackled by the self while in the other, it is resolved from the outside. Must we be independent to survive a crisis? Or can we be dependent? Can we rely on others? Can others rely on us?

Stories of the Prophets

In Jewish, Christian, and Islamic lore, themes of hopelessness and hope oscillate like a pendulum, moving one way sometimes and another the next. Adam and Eve are cast out of Eden for eating the Forbidden Fruit, but hope is sent through angels and prophets who help humanity find their way back to Paradise. There are floods, fires, and the wrath of God, as well as refuge, protection, and the love of God.

Arabic tales tell us how Hagar and Ismael, abandoned in the desert, find the waters of Zamzam to quench their thirst. Yusuf, known in the Old Testament as Joseph, is treated badly by his brothers and sold into slavery in Egypt. But he forgives them and ends up providing shelter to his entire family during a great famine.

Egyptians enslave the Hebrews, and hope appears through Prophet Moses who leads them across the wilderness and the sea to the Promised Land. Stories describe the resilience and patience of Job (Ayyub) through the worst of misfortunes and of Jonas (Yunus) rediscovering faith in the belly of a whale.

We hear of suffering in Israel, of years of prosecution, before the rise of kings who built temples to the God. Temples are destroyed and resurrected, there are exiles to Babylon and triumphant returns. Noah survives a terrifying flood by holding on to his faith.

To a humble believer, the words of Jesus Christ in the New Testament bring hope. Words of Allah, spoken to Muhammad and communicated through the Quran, inspire faith in the Muslim during dark times.

All this reveals that the experience of helplessness is not unique to us or our times. It has always been so – around the world. The characters in these stories experience death, devastation, hunger, homelessness, loneliness, and complete despair. Think of this literature as the wisdom of our ancestors that we can dip into in times of crisis.

The Ramayana and the Mahabharata

Similar stories abound in Hindu epics. In the Ramayana, Ram is told on the eve of his coronation that he has to leave the palace and go to the forest in exile for fourteen years. Imagine a situation where we are told that we will not get our inheritance for that long a time or where we are thrown into jail for fourteen years for no fault of ours. How would we feel?

At the near end of the epic, Ram's wife Sita finds herself in the forest, pregnant and abandoned by her husband. The first time in the forest when she is kidnapped by a demon and taken to the island of Lanka, she has faith that Ram will come to save her. But the very Ram casts her out of Ayodhya in the end. Wasn't Ram her guardian? How would you feel if your guardian abandoned you? Why would Valmiki narrate such a story in an epic meant to glorify Ram? What is he trying to teach us?

In the Mahabharata, Karna is abandoned by his mother and subsequently rejected by his teachers because he is low-born. The Pandavas find themselves as refugees in the forest, their palace burnt by their cousins, the Kauravas. Who do they turn to when their family has turned into their killers? Most dramatically, Draupadi is gambled away by her husbands and dragged in public, stripped of her privileges, security, honour, and her dignity.

Like Sunahshepa, she has nowhere to turn to. 'Do I turn to my husbands? But they have become mute spectators. Do I turn to the king, the one who represents the state? But the state is silent.' It's like those horrible WhatsApp videos of today, of goons surrounding people and beating them up while the police watch doing nothing. There's nobody to help the victims, nobody to come to their rescue. Neither the people watching and filming the scene nor the state, the police, not even you.

The Mahabharata contains many mini-epics, each mirroring the misery of the Pandavas and Draupadi. Take the story of Nala and Damayanti that the Pandavas hear in the forest.

Nala is a handsome king. He marries Damayanti, a woman so beautiful that even the gods want to marry her. Jealous, the gods create all kinds of problems for this couple. Nala loses his fortune and his kingdom in a gambling match. He's forced to leave his palace with his wife, with just the clothes on his body.

Nala thinks he will run a small business to make ends meet. He's a dreamer. He's always been an entitled prince, someone who has never worked a day in his life. He announces, I will catch birds in the forest and sell them in the market. And the wife says okay, but how do we catch them. He says, don't worry, I've got a dhoti. I'll use this as a trap. He has never caught birds in his life. He spreads the cloth and when the birds sit on it, he thinks he can trap them. But then the birds fly away with his dhoti, leaving the king naked. Nala sees the birds are smarter than him. His self-worth, self-esteem completely collapse. He is a man with nothing, not even a dhoti to cover him.

Damayanti tries to calm him. She tears her saree into two and tells him to wear one half. Her love and support make him feel even worse. At night when she's sleeping, unable to bear the thought that he's so useless, he runs away in the darkness. Damayanti finds herself in the middle of the forest all alone. But she is not worried about herself. She's worried for Nala. What is going to happen to him? Determined to find him, she makes a plan.

The Nala–Damayanti story shows a man who's completely shattered and the woman playing his saviour. When we talk of despair, what is the gender that comes to our mind? Most would say Sita of the Ramayana, who is abandoned by her husband Ram, the king of Ayodhya, heeding public gossip. We are conditioned to think of Sita as the archetypal character representing the plight of women. And yet, in Nala's story, it's very much the other way around.

Different responses to a crisis

After the gambling match, the five Pandava brothers must leave the city, stripped of their status and fortune. They had entered the city as kings but are doomed to leave as paupers after a single gambling match where they lost everything – wealth, power, status, property, and their dignity too. They are left with no self-esteem because they behaved like louts in the gambling hall, foolishly betting away everything they had. Bereft of all sense. They lose the respect of their people and feel ashamed of themselves.

As they leave the city, Dhritarasthra asks Vidur and his courtiers to describe how the brothers appear. It's a narrative device to help you see the emotions that run through the Pandavas. Bhima is seen massaging his muscles, warming them up as if indicating he will come back and kill Duryodhana. Draupadi stands caressing her unbound hair, reiterating her public resolve to tie it up only when she has had her vengeance. (In many folk traditions, Bhima and Draupadi are considered to be Bhairava and Bhairavi. They stand for anger and revenge.)

Nakula, the handsome Pandava adored by many women, is seen covering his face with soot and dust. There is much anger and blame among the five brothers and Draupadi in the forest. One blames the Kauravas, the other point fingers at Yudhishthira's weakness. **As you try to find explanations for the crisis that has happened, you blame fate, other people, finally even yourself.**

Draupadi's anger never ceases, nor do her quarrels. Arjuna finds he can't be with his family in such an atmosphere. He leaves them to meditate, meets his father Indra, and tries to amass weapons for the future war. He can't bear to see the face of his elder brother, whom he respects a lot. Yudhishthira tries to be graceful but his family do not allow him to stay calm.

The response in the Ramayana is different. There is Lakshman screaming and yelling, saying Kaikeyi is responsible, Bharat is responsible, our father is weak. Sita says nothing, she simply stands next to Ram, in support. Ram doesn't respond at all. Of course, he is the ideal man, a god. As humans, we are more like Lakshman than Ram. But through these stories, the tellers are trying to explain what the graceful reaction to hopelessness is while also presenting the more common, human responses to the crisis.

Hopelessness has different effects on people. Draupadi transforms herself into an angry person. She vows that she will not tie her hair until she can wash it with the blood of the Kauravas. She becomes vengeful, aggressive, and is always portrayed with her hair unbound. It's a very violent image but also a glamorous one because Draupadi glistens and shimmers in her rage. Those who made me feel helpless, I shall do the same to them. I will avenge myself when the opportunity is right. Revenge in this case manifests as hope. Draupadi believes revenge will end her sense of despair.

Contrast this with Sita in the Ramayana where there is no fantasy of revenge. I have always observed that people glamorize revenge in our storytelling. We don't like characters who are not vengeful. Sita seems boring when compared to Draupadi, with no unbound hair, no eyes flashing fire, no fiery dialogues.

It's significant that Valmiki tells us that Sita is the daughter of Janak of Mithila. She's born of a king who is associated with the Upanishads, the Vedic doctrines of self-reflection and self-realization. Now, this is a very important aspect to remember. She is the daughter of a very wise man. That's a code.

By calling Sita the daughter of Janak, the author is telling us that this is a person whose response is going to be based on wisdom. Draupadi is raw and elemental, born of fire. She emerges as an adult. She has no mother. By contrast, Sita has had a childhood, she is born of earth and raised by a foster father who is an extremely erudite man. She's surrounded by sages through her childhood.

If Draupadi's response to despair is anger, Sita's is disappointment followed by acceptance. The Ram who saved her from Ravana's Lanka was her husband and guardian. The Ram who abandoned her was Ayodhya's king, scion of the Raghu clan, leader of the solar dynasty, who valued royal reputation over marriage and family.

If I had to imagine Sita's state of mind in the forest when she is left behind by her husband, I would visualize this: the first moment, there is shock, and horror, and despair. But soon she would think, 'Let me find food, let me find water. I have life inside my body, I'm pregnant. I will have to feed them.' As she is consumed by the practicalities of life, she would be more analytical about her circumstances.

In the Nala–Damayanti story, we are led

into the story of a man who is in the throes of a complete breakdown. Nala is seen falling in a downward spiral, triggered by misfortune, and Damayanti clinging to him, trying to pull him out. She's the one stretching out her hand to pull the drowning Nala out of the maelstrom. She is the Vishnu rescuing the elephant-king. In Sita's story, she has to fight the crab herself. No one will come to her rescue.

Ram is helpless too, bound by royal rules. The mother of his children is in the forest, and he cannot do anything to take care of them. We imagine that Sita must have lived comfortably with the sages in a sylvan retreat. But in the folk songs in Telugu, her life in the forest is described as harsh as she struggles to provide food for her children and protect them from the wilderness. It must have been a tough life as a single mother. Born a princess, Sita would not have imagined that she would face such eventualities after marriage, that too after supporting her husband through his worst time.

So we find these stories moving into different emotions: from helplessness some move into vengeance as in the case of Draupadi, some like Nala wish to just hide and disappear from the world. Then there is Ram bound by unfair rules, holding on to his dignity and the principles of kingship, while Sita focuses on practicalities, not judging Ram.

In the face of death

Ram as a king encounters a father in front of his palace, holding his dead child. The grieving father says, 'I thought in Ram Rajya, everything would be predictable, fathers would die before sons. But here is my son, lying in my lap. Should a father have to ever witness the death of his child? Is that orderly? Is this Ram Rajya?' It's a very moving image because you see that Ram is unable to do anything about it. The king has been shown his place. Ram may be god on earth, but even he has to accept the rules of the earth and submit to the reality of death.

A similar story is found in the Mahabharata where Arjuna the great warrior says, 'I can defeat every monster.' Krishna takes Arjuna to a young couple in distress. 'Every time their baby is born, it dies. Can you keep death away so that they can have a child?' he asks. Arjuna builds a fortress of arrows, ready to kill Yama, the god of death. But he cannot, the child is again born dead. In front of death, even the greatest of heroes fade into nothing.

In the Stree Parva of the Mahabharata, when all the soldiers are dead, there is a powerful description of the women flooding into the battlefield, wailing for their sons and husbands and brothers. Gandhari, weeping for her hundred sons, curses Krishna bitterly. 'You are supposed to be divine. What have you done? You didn't spare a single child of mine.' Gandhari blames Krishna and the Pandavas. Not once does she hold her children responsible for not settling for peace when it was within their power.

In the face of death, we wonder what's the point of it all. But the world continues silently, whether we find meaning or not. The world exists. It owes us no explanation.

I think Krishna is the most helpless character in the Mahabharata. Because here is the most powerful man who cannot stop a war and prevent the death of millions. Even the god on earth cannot convince the Kauravas to make peace. Stories such as these remind us there is no escape from hopelessness, even for the divine. We have to submit to the harsh realities of life. Not everything is in our control.

Think of Krishna walking away from the Kaurava court after negotiations fail. God could not stop the Kauravas from fighting the Pandavas. And he could not convince the Pandavas to not hate the Kauravas. He said to them, 'You can fight for your wealth, I can understand that, but why do you hate them? Don't confuse fairness with revenge.'

But who heard what Krishna said? We think Krishna promotes revenge and rage when he supports Draupadi but he does nothing to save her children who die in the war that enables her to finally tie her hair, drenched in the blood of her enemies. Everybody is angry and upset, despite being none the wiser.

In the Mahabharata, Krishna dies alone in the forest, after witnessing his own family, the Yadav clan, fighting and killing each other at Prabhas Teerth. He was not able to stop the war between the Pandavas and the Kauravas. Now he's not able to stop the war between the two factions of his own family. All his talk on dharma and living together peaceably falls on deaf ears. His brother Balaram is bitter and angry with him and walks away. A hunter aims, mistaking him for an animal. The poison spreads through his body slowly. The world continues as before.

Can we change the world? Krishna before dying gives his final discourse to Uddhava, his old friend. Many of those teachings are the same as in the Bhagavad Gita, which he narrates before the war breaks between the Kauravas and Pandavas. We find the same ideas in the Upanishads. These are considered Sanatan and Shaswat, timeless ideas that will not change. It is the foundation of Hindu wisdom. Krishna is not bitter despite his apparent failure to prevent wars. Why? Should he not be frustrated?

Shouldn't the Ramayana and the Mahabharata end in triumph, a glorious climax? Yet, the stories end as tragedies. And in these tragedies, the gods on earth, Ram, Sita, and Krishna, are visualized as calm and graceful. Krishna is even envisioned as a cherubic cosmic child, cradled by a leaf on stormy waters, ready to experience life once more with the same enthusiasm as before.

There must be a lesson here, which we will unravel in the next four chapters.

2

Why do we hope?

We feel hopeless because hope exists. We feel helpless because we expect to be helped. We have hope and seek help because we are humans, and as humans we hear stories about gods and heroes who offer hope as well as assistance. The purpose of society is to protect us from the harsh realities of nature where there are no angels, guardians, or gods, no demons either.

In this chapter, we will explore the origins of hope. We will explore:

- Whether plants and animals live in a world of hope, and how they negotiate between abundance and scarcity in predictable and unpredictable circumstances.
- How different mythologies describe abundance and what the term means.

- Why we expect to get everything, to have abundance in our lives.

The point of this chapter is to make us realize that **hope is essential to the human condition, which is why we need to manufacture it all the time and cling to it despite all adversities.**

Scarcity is nature's reality

Most resources in this world are scarce. They are not available to everyone in equal quantities. **Our idea of abundance arises from our most primal memories of scarcity.** Those that we hoard in our amygdala, the oldest part of our brain.

Do animals live in abundance? Do plants? Plants live by getting water deep within the soil using their roots, and they gather as much energy as they want from the sun. The water dries up in summer, and then they wait for the rains to come. Sunlight disappears at night or on cloudy days. In winter, sunlight exists for just a few hours. So plants are constantly struggling for life.

Then there are the rivals. Other plants too want that water, and that sunlight, and those nutrients. This struggle is most evident in dense rainforests with plants climbing on top of each other, claiming the light, leaving competitors in the shadows. There are parasites that feed on the nutrients collected by other plants. This is nature's silent war – well documented by botanists.

The same is true of animals too. They are continually struggling for pastures, for prey. There is not enough grass to eat, never enough animals to eat. The deer runs too fast for the leopard. The lions have to strategize well to catch the weakest buffalo. The tiger, the hyena, the elephant all have to keep walking in search of food. Birds have to migrate vast distances, across seas and mountains and continents, for warm weather and food. Look at the polar bear. Every time it walks, the ground shakes, and every seal knows that there is a predator on the prowl. The bear must stand in the cold, patiently waiting for the prey to come within its reach.

Besides, nothing is predictable. There are

droughts, floods, epidemics, and forest fires. A single virus can mutate and wipe out a species. Many creatures live on the edge of extinction, many face starvation. There is never enough food. And always more mouths to feed. The strongest may get a full meal, but most starve. The deer does not eat a full belly as that prevents it from running when the tiger attacks. And the tiger is always lurking in the corner. If not the tiger, then the viper, or the scorpion.

Think of turtles hatching out of their eggs on a sandy beach, making their way towards the sea. As they slowly move towards their new watery home, a flock of birds swoop down to grab them. And that's life for the little turtle babies. They live in a dangerous world without any protector. They have survived the incubation period, when they could have been eaten by snakes. They are now going into the sea where on the way they might be eaten by birds or killed or captured by humans. If they are lucky they get to the water, the deep dark unknown.

Plants and animals don't have anyone to complain to. They don't have a state with whom they have a social contract. They can't go to their leader and say that you have not provided for us. The reason why the elephant matriarch is respected is that she has lived the longest. Therefore, in drought, she is most likely to remember where the waterholes are. You matter only if you help others survive.

Our lower brain holds these evolutionary memories of scarcity, of scraping through existence, of making just enough to survive. A time when there were only a few months of abundance in spring and summer. And then winter returned. Nature doesn't make it easy.

For all animals, starvation is one hunt away, one meal away. A forest fire can come and destroy you. The world was equally uncertain and dangerous for early humans. Nature gives you just enough resources to survive. You don't have an excess of resources because it destroys the balance of the ecosystem. If one animal has more resources than the other, then something goes wrong in the food chain. Nature is almost conservative in providing resources.

So when humans came along and started

composing stories, we made up stories of permanent abundance. Eden is one such place of everlasting abundance. Not just a place with overflowing food, but one where we don't have to work for food and where food is always guaranteed.

Animals have to work for food. In Mesopotamian mythology, gods created humans so that they would work and the gods could relax. In Greek mythology, the gods do not have to work for ambrosia. In Hindu mythology, the devas live in abundance. Our ancient gods are like the way we describe the rich and the famous today.

Humans sought excess resources so that they had to never think of starvation. That desire propelled the agricultural revolution more than ten thousand years ago. That's why we started herding animals. That's why we built granaries and eventually shaped the industrial revolution about two hundred years ago. These actions were all done to generate abundance. **But is it possible to make abundance for everyone all the time?**

The many myths of abundance

Myths are the subjective truth of a people. Different cultures have diverse myths. But we find a common pattern in most. **All people, in different ways, imagine a world of abundance – a world of no scarcity. It's called heaven.**

In Greek mythology, the gods live on Mount Olympus, enjoying their lives, drinking ambrosia, eating from the magical goat horn, cornucopia, which overflows with fruits and flowers.

In Norse mythology, we hear of magical goats that eat from the Tree of Life and whose milk is the nectar of immortality. These goats can be killed, and their meat, eaten. But if their bones are preserved, they come back to life the next day, ready to provide for another meal. Thus, there is an eternal supply to satisfy our hunger.

In Swarga, heaven in Indian mythology, described in Buddhist, Jain, and Hindu lore, we encounter the wish-fulfilling tree Kalpataru, the wish-fulfilling cow Kamadhenu. There is Chintamani or the wish-fulfilling gem and Akshay Patra, a pot overflowing with gold and grains. These are the treasures of the universe churned from the ocean of milk found in the paradise of the devas. This paradise is the realm of abundance. The gods have everything we desire. They can get everything by just asking for it. No effort is needed.

Descriptions of Jannat, heaven in Islamic thought, also allude to a world where the faithful are always young and every individual owns palaces with gardens and fountains and fruits of every kind. Where there is no hunger, no wants. Not even old age or bad breath. There are celestial beings who will satisfy every need of the faithful. No need to work. Just rest, enjoy, and indulge all desires, for eternity.

The universal nature of these stories makes us realize that **humans dream of a world where they do not have to work, where they always feel strong and surrounded by opportunities. There is no threat, no weakness, no anxiety, no fear, no rival, no predator.** Isn't that what politicians promise in their speeches election after election? Is that not why we follow leaders? To go to the

Promised Land of milk and honey, of freedom and dignity?

Humans created the nation-state to realize the myth of abundance. How old are the nation-states? Less than two hundred years and the process carved out the entire planet into nearly two hundred nations. This nation-state, if we follow its rules, promises to give us social security – jobs, pensions, healthcare, education, proper infrastructure. This is the social contract theory. In developed economies, the state says when we are still young and dependent, if our parents are not good enough, the state will take care of us. When we are old and our children don't take care of us, the state will take care of us.

So essentially, through the state, we manufacture our idea of god – the all-powerful but just, and a source of all opportunities. In China, the emperor was supposed to create heaven on earth. The Communist Party of China's creation of the social order is, in effect, a move towards realizing this ancient promise. Being a citizen of a state thus gives us hope.

When a state does not take care of its citizens, it is projected as a 'false' god and we seek the true god, a state that is concerned about its citizens, does not entertain social inequality, and ensures the environment is not polluted by human greed. We migrate to such a state that offers greater hope. Just like the ancient people who abandoned gods who did not help them in favour of gods who did.

But can we expect abundance for everyone?

When our myths talk of abundance, they also talk about how it's only for a few. The gods have it, but humans don't in Mesopotamian mythology. If the humans who exist to work so that the gods can relax serve well, they may be given entrance to paradise after death.

In the Bible, humans would have always enjoyed abundance and remained in paradise had they just listened to God and not eaten the forbidden fruit. The prophets of the Abrahamic religions bring with them the laws of God that people have to obey if they hope to return to Eden.

In Hindu mythology, the paradise of the devas is constantly under siege because the asuras want to take away what the devas want. As a contrast to the Swarga-of-abundance is the Naraka-of-scarcity.

Jain mythology talks about Lok Purusha; it is how Jains imagine space. As you go higher and higher, you come to the world of greater abundance, Swarga. And as you go lower, you reach a place of greater and greater scarcity, which is Naraka. This idea is represented in board games invented by Jain monks – snakes and ladders. Snakes pull us down to Naraka where we experience hunger. The ladders pull us up to Swarga where there is all the food we want.

So our oldest stories point to our desire for a perfect place where life will be without sadness and strife but will remind us continually that it's nearly impossible. There is also an ethical and moral layer to this abundance–scarcity divide. We are told the devas in Swarga are good and obedient. They participate in yagnas, the ritual of exchange. Those who are out of paradise are bad and disobedient. They reject the ritual of exchange. So good karma provides food and bad karma generates starvation. In a way, these stories seem to justify the wealth of the rich and the poverty of the poor. The rich are rich because they performed the right rituals; the poor are poor because they did not.

Scarcity is linked in the mythologies to disobedience or not aligning with the gods. If you are aligned with the gods, you are in tune with the divine, you will always be in abundance. When you displease the gods, you fall from abundance to the world of scarcity. This is a recurring theme in all mythologies. Biblical (including Islamic) lore highlight this. Cities like Sodom, Gomorrah, Thamud, and Ad reject God's way and so are destroyed by floods, fire, winds, earthquakes, and volcanoes.

The Mahabharata tells the story of King Nahusha who is invited to the heavens. When he's in heaven, he wants to sit in a palanquin and be carried by all the sages. Because heaven satisfies all wishes, his too is granted. Inevitably, he treats them like he treats any servant and insults them. The rishis are enraged and say, 'You are not deserving of heaven' and he tumbles down in the form of a python waiting for its food with its mouth perpetually open.

In the nineteenth century, we saw the rise of the Communist ideology. Here the rich were the oppressors and the poor, the oppressed. It reflected the biblical ideas of God telling Moses to stand up against the mighty pharaoh of Egypt on behalf of the Hebrew slaves. Good was now equated with the oppressed. Obedience and loyalty were good, provided they were to the Communist ideology that challenged the rich and the powerful. In the new political thought, poverty was the result of the rich being unfair, not the poor being disobedient, as believed in the old feudal thought. Scarcity was no longer linked to disobedience but to corruption and greed.

So our hope that the world will be a better place depends on two ideas: everyone aligns with the common law for the common good (whatever that might be) or the rich and the powerful become more generous and kind, and stop exploiting the poor and the powerless. These are huge expectations for a planet of over seven billion people divided into 200 independent nation-states. It is like trying to boil the ocean.

Happily ever after?

The great story that illustrates some of these ideas and tensions comes from the Puranas – the story of the cosmic Amrut Manthan, the churning of the ocean of milk. This story even became popular in Southeast Asian temples, taken there by sea-merchants from India trading in cloth and spices over a thousand years ago.

In the story, the devas and the asuras are at loggerheads with each other as resources are scarce and they decide to churn the ocean of milk together. If you start making a list of all the things that materialize from the ocean of milk, you will realize what emerges is abundance and affluence. Trees, cows, horses, elephants, jewellery, singers, dancers, the moon, and wine.

Everything that makes life wonderful. But the devas trick the asuras and take away everything. Thereafter, the asuras keep fighting the devas to get their share of the bargain. The fight is never-ending. The devas are unable to enjoy their paradise as it is constantly under siege.

The deva–asura conflict takes place because the distribution was not fair. Swarga is created by the goods that should have been shared with the asuras. So, **inherent in the idea of abundance is that someone has been stripped of their fair share.** The devas become the haves and the asuras, the have-nots. Yet, as children, we are told the devas are good and fair, besides being slim and beautiful while the asuras are bad and dark, fat and ugly.

The Puranas speak of how Shiva, Vishnu, and Devi help the devas by defeating the asuras. But the asuras keep coming back – regenerating themselves with sanjivani vidya. Shiva, Vishnu, and Devi are the 'high gods' of Hinduism while the devas are the 'low gods'. What is the difference? The high gods have conquered hunger and are trying to teach the devas that happiness lies not in the pursuit of food but the conquest of hunger. As long as they corner all the wealth in Swarga, they will always be fighting the asuras. There will be no happily ever after.

That is something that we often don't notice. Because when we are in abundance, we don't realize the ecosystem beyond abundance. That one person's abundance often comes at the cost of another's. We do not notice that electricity has gone in the neighbourhood, until our electricity goes off.

The gods have abundance but the humans don't, the devas have abundance but the asuras don't. There is abundance in Eden for those who are obedient, but none for those who are disobedient. So there is this constant struggle with abundance. Even in our fantasies of abundance, we recognize that it is not universal or permanent.

Abundance can be permanent, as in the Islamic Jannat, provided everyone in the world is aligned with God, obeys the rules of the state, universally submits unconditionally to a higher power. But no matter how hard we try, everyone will not think the same way – because we are human.

God may be the shepherd, but all humans will not be sheep. Some will choose to be goats and wolves. Sheep see the shepherd as god because the shepherd takes care of them, but the wolf and goat prefer to take care of themselves.

The metaphor of the good shepherd makes us feel safe, that someone will take care of us. But shepherds herd sheep for their wool and meat, don't they? Our heart is constantly broken by those in whom we have the greatest trust. Experience teaches us the divine, the rich, and the powerful will break our hearts and not keep their end of the bargain. We can be good, righteous, obedient all our life, but abundance can still be out of reach, especially when we need it the most. And that is traumatic.

Modern secular societies function very much like old religious societies. Only God, who is all-powerful and just and who demands obedience, is replaced by the all-powerful and just state. Europe and America tell citizens that if they follow the democratic process, the state will take care of everything. China tells its citizens that it will take away their freedom, and isolate them from the world with a firewall, but in exchange will provide for them. This is the social contract. This gives hope.

The state is the good shepherd, taking care of the weakest sheep. If we follow the rules, pay taxes, respect value, we expect the shepherd to take care of us during an emergency. When the shepherd fails to help us, when the ambulance does not arrive on time, when the hospital does not offer a bed that we paid for, when the insurance denies us treatment, we feel betrayed.

As children, we take abundance for granted. Even in the mother's womb, the child will take all the nutrients from the mother, even at the cost of the mother. Nature will always prefer the child over the parent. When the child is born, they are prioritized because they are the next generation. Even in the poorest household, everything is done to ensure the child gets food and comfort. Or else the child will die. But then we grow up – cast out of the womb, the cradle, the affectionate arms of the parent. We are cast out of Eden. We have to fend for ourselves.

The Mongols took this idea and turned it around. Apparently, to make children tough, Mongols would always keep the elders closer to the fire and the younger people (not the babies cradled in the mothers' arms) further away. The children had to fight their way for comfort, and that made them aggressive. This is what happens in societies with fewer opportunities. When there is less, people become more aspirational.

We live in an era of growth and development. We are constantly told that the world will get better and better. The internet will solve all our problems. If we go to school and study hard, we will get a job and when we get a job or even start our enterprise, life will be better. Today's fashionable stories are of heroic narratives of things not working out for people who then struggle to find a solution. Business books about how people break the rules and become successful are written every day. Even the Ramayana and the Mahabharata are narrated as if moving towards a climax. When in fact, the old stories in most traditions are very different.

Some stories are shaped like a wave suggesting

things will get better and worse. You hope that it begins in a bad place and ends in a good place. But that's not always the case. The Ramayana ends not in the death of Ravana but the exile of Sita. The Mahabharata ends not with the defeat of the Kauravas but the Pandavas encountering Naraka. Puranic stories end not with the defeat of the asuras, but with the reminder that a new asura will re-emerge.

Some are cyclical stories, like the Vikram and Vetal story, where Vetal tells Vikramaditya a story and asks him to solve a puzzle and the moment he solves it, the Vetal flies back to the tree. Vikramaditya has to go back to the tree, pick him up, and try to bring him to the sorcerer each time. These stories remind us that life is cyclical, the same thing happens again and again.

So there are different ways of telling stories where they can be cyclical narrations, wave-like, or they can have a clear arc with a definite ending. But what is happening in the world today is that one is being privileged over the other. The idea is that the world will get to a better place. It's the politician telling us that good things will happen in the future, just let this particular industry be built and all the problems will be solved.

This is what I call the 'Western' narrative, which is always talking about the world getting better and better and if it is not improving, we will need a revolution. The activist discourse of revolutions on the one side, and the capitalist discourse on the other that says once we have enough structures, policies, resources, and wealth in place, life will get better. So we have these two schools of thought battling each other.

On the one side is the discourse of development and growth – that life will be better when technology and wealth come into our life. And on the other is this thought that life is unfair and unjust, and we have to revolt and fight and scream and shout. Both of them promise us that one day the world will get better.

Is there no third kind of story? **Is it possible that at this moment there are people who are happy, and there are people who are sad? That's how the world will always be. We are all on waves going through multiple cycles. And our life itself will go through waves, up and down** and up and down. Those below feel miserable but why do those with abundance feel threatened and anxious? It makes one wonder if abundance and scarcity are simply subjective truths, myths, indifferent to objective, measurable, observable reality.

3

Where does hopelessness come from?

In the Upanishads, our body is called deha. Atma is dehi, the resident of the human body. Atma is the soul that never dies, so it never experiences any scarcity or fear. Atma is the eternal witness, forever tranquil. What experiences scarcity and fear, what dies is only the body.

This body is not simply our flesh. It is also our mind. It is also the world around us – culture, nature, the plants, animals, and humans who live around us. Just as we cannot remove our mind from our body, we cannot remove our body from the ecosystem it inhabits. The mind seeks to control the body, as well as the world around it. But it fails. The body decays and degenerates despite all efforts of the mind. Despite many inventions and innovations, the world outside us remains unpredictable. This is the source of hopelessness.

Having acknowledged hopelessness as a natural human reaction in chapter 1, and hope as a natural human need for opportunities in chapter 2, let us look at the source of hopelessness in greater detail. In this chapter we will learn about:

- The architecture of the world as presented in the Hindu scriptures: a series of concentric circles or mandalas, comprising nature, culture, and the mind; how the mind creates a subjective world distinct from the objective world outside of us.
- How with time, although our control over nature and culture seems to have increased, we still cannot control the subjective world.
- Why the same objective situation can create different subjective responses, one that brings hope and the other that brings hopelessness.
- The tragic story of Drona.
- How even abundance cannot prevent us from feeling discontented or bored, thus sowing seeds of crisis.

- How the subjective truth of fatalism (we are helpless) fares against the subjective truth of determinism (we are in charge).

This chapter is diagnostic, after which chapters 4 and 5 will proceed to discuss how to handle a crisis in the immediate and long term.

The three worlds we live in

Monotheistic religions like Christianity and Islam begin with the story of creation: God created the world. There was nothing before. This idea spread around the world from the fifth century when the Roman Empire became Christian. This view is challenged by the Big Bang Theory of science. The theory denies the role of something intelligent in the act of creation. However, it does seem to agree with biblical myths that life started from nothingness.

But creation in Hindu, Buddhist, and Jain traditions is not just objective. It is also subjective. The Upanishads talk of Prajapati as the creator. He is born of a lotus, which means the lotus pre-exists him. And when he emerges, he becomes self-aware.

In self-awareness, he experiences loneliness and therefore seeks companionship. He's hungry, and therefore seeks food. He's frightened and therefore seeks comfort and security. He becomes curious, he gets bored, he creates amusements. He realizes he needs others around him, he needs relationships. This shatters his self-containment. He becomes needy. Creation is thus linked to the mind, the creator creates out of desire and need.

The world is thus not just nature, it is also the human mind, which creates culture. Cultures come and go, nature remains forever, and the human mind responds to both in different ways.

Indian scriptures teach us that there are three worlds we all occupy. The natural world, prakriti, that all plants and animals, including us, share. **Nature is indifferent to humans. It does not care for humans, but it does respond to everything that we do, not intelligently but in a reactionary way.**

We occupy a social world, sanskriti, which is created by humans who domesticate nature. Society exists only because we have imagined within ourselves a better life through brahmanda, which is the personal reality of each individual.

You have a personal reality that was born with you and will die with you. This is true for every individual. There are as many brahmandas as there are humans. Animals don't have it, humans have it. Humans come together to create sanskriti, which is culture.

You and I may or may not share the same culture, but we all share nature. However, we never share our own personal reality located in the mind – the source of all our problems and solutions. Thus, value is placed on the mind in Indian thought, over ideas like God (dominant in Western mythology) and nature (dominant in Chinese mythology).

Why is this important? It's important because when we talk of hopelessness, we must ask ourselves – is it coming from nature, is it coming from culture, is it coming from our imagination? **Where do our sadness and despair** come from? Is hope a natural phenomenon or a cultural construction? Where is it coming from? Is it objective or subjective?

The source of our despair

How do animals react when they are suddenly faced with a calamity? They are traumatized, they are stressed, they are frightened. But when the stress has passed, they go about living their life. Animals and plants do not have anyone to complain to. Humans do.

We have an insatiable urge to make the world a better place. So we invent tools and technologies. We establish laws and societies with leaders and regulatory bodies. We imagine gods and even one all-powerful God. These human creations are answerable to humans.

Humans have the faculty of imagination. We can imagine a better life, a happily-ever-after life. And that's the source of both our creativity and our stress. And because we can always imagine an alternative reality, we become unhappy. We can innovate and invent things to make the world better or mourn the fact that development has not been achieved. Imagination never lets the world be perfect. There is always something better still to be achieved.

Let's look at the Ramayana and the Mahabharata to understand this. Both refer to a forest exile. Ram goes to the forest, so do the Pandavas. Ram is never shown complaining when he is told to go to the forest, while the Pandavas are always portrayed as angry and upset.

One day, the Pandavas visit the great sage Markandeya. Markandeya looks at Yudhishthira and says you are unhappy that you have been told to go to the forest for thirteen years. Let me tell you the story of a prince who went to the jungle for fourteen years, so a year more than your exile, and he narrates the Ramopakhyan, which is the older version of the Ramayana embedded in the Mahabharata.

As he narrates Ram's tale, Markandeya says that the prince suffered for no fault of his. He was a victim of politics between his father and mother. In your case, Yudhishthira, you have created the mishap yourself. Ram never complained. That brings us to the idea of objective and subjective. Everybody faces crises. Will we all handle a crisis in the same way? How does one prince handle it differently from the other and why?

Sometimes objective contexts have to be considered to make sense of subjective emotions. The rich and the poor can both experience hunger – but when we consider the objective premise, the two hungers become different. The hunger of the rich in abundance is different from the hunger of the poor in scarcity. The former's hunger manifests as ambition and greed. While the hunger of the poor is characterized by aspiration and need.

A child is not able to go to school because there is no school in the village. That's one problem. Another kind of problem is where a parent feels the worst calamity in the world has happened because her child does not go to the best school, like the children of her friends.

When the school is shut down due to COVID-19, we can blame nature. When the school authorities argue about opening schools, we have entered the realm of culture – we can find blame in the many arguments about school fees and risks of reopening. But then comes our own personal response to our children studying at home, away from social interaction, away from friends. How do we respond to this fact? Is the stress we face due to the given situation or due to our response to it?

Today, everyone is selling hope. The iPhone is selling hope that a better camera will change your life, body deodorants are selling hope that your body fragrance will attract the opposite sex. Communists are selling us the hope of justice and equality. We are growing up with the idea that one day the world will get better. We are never told that the world is good, here and now, that things can get bad in the land of abundance and worse in the land of scarcity.

Technology, political doctrines, and economic status will change over time, but jealousy will always be there everywhere, no matter what. Emotions of anger, frustration, yearning are timeless and universal. As they focus greatly on these mental modifications or vikaras, Hinduism, Buddhism, and Jainism often refer to themselves as sanatan dharma (timeless faith). This is how the Ramayana and the Mahabharata are to be understood, not through the objective lens, perceiving them as historical facts, but through the subjective lens, which help us to see them as timeless and universal.

Yes, we have cell phones and nuclear weapons, more stuff than our ancestors ever had. We cannot be sent into 'forest exile' but we cannot stop cousins from being jealous of us, other men wanting our wives, husbands being unfaithful. This truth of the subjective realm is constant. We live emotional lives within material ecosystems.

Change in material circumstances does not change us emotionally. Rich people experience frustration and heartbreak and so do the poor. In the past, we could die of typhoid or a flood would wash us away. Today we can be felled by COVID-19, or a tsunami, or the collapse of a building like the condo that fell down in the USA recently. We may die in different ways, but we are as much prey to unplanned events, to heartbreak, and tragedies as we were in the past.

Today, right now in the Sundarbans, there are people who know that when the rains come, their mud houses will be wiped out, and they will have to build anew yet again. They want pucca houses but the politicians never keep their promise. People will get on with their lives until the crisis strikes again.

Meanwhile, someone in Scandinavia feels threatened that the arriving Muslim immigrants will change his society forever. He is filled with dread and despair at the thought of the world around him changing. If we look at life from a subjective viewpoint rather than objective, we realize we are no different from our ancestors.

I don't know what challenges my grandfather went through. But I do know that his life would have had strengths, weaknesses, opportunities, and threats. I have those in my life, you have them too, your child will also have them, we all will. Just because we have more technology and resources does not mean that jealousy has decreased, hatred has disappeared, and people are smarter and wiser.

Ravana was a Vedic scholar, had immense wealth and power, many wives, and still he desired Sita, still he found no other way to get justice for his sister whose nose was cut by Lakshman except by stealing another man's wife. The Kauravas could easily have shared their wealth with their five cousins, but they chose to go to war.

Are we wiser? Has technology changed the cruelty quotient in the world? **Are we less cruel today because we have cell phones? Prakriti may be domesticated, sanskriti may be controlled, but brahmanda defies restraint.** Here lies the primary source of hopelessness and hope.

What's really in our control?

Drona was extremely poor; he couldn't feed his family. That's a real crisis. He goes to his rich friend, a king called Drupada, and asks for a cow. His friend insults him. Drona is hurt and decides to avenge his insult.

Drupada is as educated as Drona. Both studied together. One is rich, one is poor. Both lack the grace to deal with scarcity and poverty. Poor Drona looks at rich Drupada, ignores the present reality, and presumes nothing has changed, and so behaves in an overly familiar manner, reminding him of childhood promises when both had agreed to share everything forever.

'We were friends, we always shared things then,' says Drona. Drupada, rather than understanding where Drona is coming from, gets offended and outraged at the presumption and declares they are not equal. And that friendship can exist only among equals.

This incident leads to a series of actions and reactions. In Hindu philosophy, action is karma, and reaction is also karma. The objective incident and the subjective response, both are karma.

Drona tells Drupada, 'I will teach you a lesson. I will take away half your kingdom.' He goes to Parshuram and learns the art of warfare. Parshuram agrees to teach him but on one condition. He should not teach the art to a Kshatriya or a royal. But the first thing Drona does is to teach it to the Kauravas and the Pandavas and uses his students to capture and claim half of Drupada's land.

An angry Drupada vows to teach Drona a lesson. He produces a daughter who marries the Pandavas and causes a split in the Kuru household. His son beheads Drona. Drona's son then kills the children of the Pandavas and the killer of his father. Thus, the Mahabharata war, where millions die, starts because two friends did not behave gracefully towards each other. They did not respect objective realities and their subjective interpretation of incidents were so warped that it fuelled great violence, harming countless people.

All this for a cow? Drona let that single incident shape his entire life. When a crisis is past, what happens to us? Do we carry it with us in our heads, in our mind? Do we still remember those hateful things our friends, or parents, or teachers said all those years ago?

I get very annoyed when I hear people give motivational talks saying 'my father was so poor and I didn't have anything' or writers talk of how their manuscripts were rejected by so many editors. This is part of life. We live in a complex system. Failure is part of life, not a reason to hate the world, or be vengeful. We just have to keep at it – because life is about striving to grab at opportunities. Does the tiger get upset when it fails to catch a deer? Does it write poetry about the hopelessness of life? Or does it simply focus on the next hunt?

The objective world is what it is. It is the subjective world, our mind and our response to the outside world, which transforms it into a set of opportunities and threats. Remember, the sun was shining for millions of years before the first tree appeared on the earth. That first tree saw sunlight as food and chased it, producing more leaves to grab more sunlight. Had they not been plants, sunlight would not have been seen as an opportunity.

Likewise, our needs establish opportunities and threats. Drona's need for food created the hero who helped him and the villain who hurt him. If Drona had had no scarcity, then he would never have fought with Drupada. If Drona had tolerated Drupada's rudeness, then he would not have become a vengeful man. Should the source of his rage, and the wars that followed, be located in objective reality (Drupada's rudeness) or subjective reality (Drona's hurt)?

Can we control the outside world or the inside world? We cannot control a publisher from rejecting our manuscript but we can control turning that rejection into the seed of despair and hopelessness, to be narrated in every literary festival, to gain sympathy, and to transform ourselves into heroes in a big bad world.

The human mind is amazingly malleable and adaptable and can create boundaries and walls so easily. We don't use the power of the mind enough. We talk about yoga, but yoga is not just a series of exercises that makes our body agile. It also makes the mind agile.

The technical definition of yoga, which emerged centuries ago, has to do with the disentangling of the knots in the mind. It's not about the body at all. It looks at the body as coagulated mind. Your entire body is seen as the mind that has become physical. What your body feels goes into your mind. Everything your mind feels is expressed in the body. In Hindu philosophy, matter is just coagulated mind.

Where does hopelessness come from?

The texts continuously talk about the psychological realm.

Our mind transforms nature into opportunities and threats, we argue what is a problem and what is a solution, we organize what we experience as strengths and weaknesses. What one mind sees as a solution, another mind sees as a problem. For example, one set of humans may see a mountain as a source of minerals that can provide metals for our society. Another set may see mining as dangerous and polluting.

For one, mining is good as it brings the promise of jobs and resources. For another, mining is bad as it can destroy the land and the rivers. For one, ban on mining creates hopelessness. For another, ban on mining creates hope. Good and bad, right and wrong, which create so much hope and hopelessness, are more subjective than objective. Lawyers can turn any violence into an act of defence or an act of offence. They can turn an act of consent into an act of violation, or vice versa.

We all have knots in our mind. Knots are born of viewing life as a set of crises. The whole purpose of this book is to enable those who read it to figure out the knots in their mind and to unknot them gently. Turn problems into opportunities, accept failure as part of life, and see crisis in context, not personally. Yoga helps us figure out what is in our control and what is not. What we can control and what we cannot. Yoga helps us give ourselves permission to let go, and not see it is as 'giving up'.

Boredom and the end of contentment

In the Puranas, the asuras do tapasya or austerities to gain powers. They aspire to conquer Swarga. The devas on the other hand are bored and entertain themselves with song and dance, in turn growing complacent. Thus, forces are at work to destroy the status quo.

That's how stories always start, right? The ambition of Kaikeyi in the Ramayana and of Satyavati in the Mahabharata. This ambition is rooted in taking what others have. In other words, it is rooted in jealousy. Both want their sons to become kings.

Then we hear of a bored king who goes on a deer hunt, behaves overconfidently, and accidentally shoots a human, stirring a whole string of unfortunate events. Dasharatha kills Shravan Kumar in the Ramayana. Pandu shoots Kindama Rishi in the Mahabharata. Actions have consequences. And from consequences come the stories – the tragedies and triumphs that fascinate us.

Abundance creates boredom, not contentment. We get irritated, and we yearn for new challenges. In satisfying this need, we often risk abundance. Like a married man or woman seeking the thrill of an extramarital affair. Or a rich man wanting to gamble, to feel the excitement of losing it all, and pulling back from the precipice.

Wherefrom comes the call for adventure? The richest in the world should be the laziest and most content, but they usually work the hardest: if not generating more wealth, then striving hard to enjoy that wealth with a vengeance. They seek the best party, the most luxurious vacation, or a place in the list of the rich and famous. At the heart is boredom, which abundance cannot take away. It's like going to the fridge and eating junk food even when we're not hungry.

Indra builds himself a palace and then says it is not good enough. He asks Vishwakarma, the architect, to build him another one. Every palace that Vishwakarma builds for him, Indra says it is not good enough. Indra may be the lord of all the damsels in the world, and yet he is drawn to the beautiful wives of the rishis. There is always something else to desire.

Abundance in the objective world does not mean abundance in the subjective world. The devas in Swarga are never content enough to be generous. The presence of abundant food does not satisfy hunger, so we choose to store rather than share. We want more – qualitatively, quantitatively. We will never be content. There is never enough. It's an idea that we need to remind ourselves.

Kuber, the lord of treasures who has all the wealth in the world, is usually depicted sitting with Shiva in his abode. The irony is very interesting because Shiva destroys hunger, and Kuber is the god of wealth. What will make us happy – the end of desires, or the fulfilment of desires? The former is pursued by hermits; the latter is sought by householders.

I wonder if the presence of a lot of food will take hunger away. Or will it just amplify it because we will want more food, better food, interesting food endlessly. Should the strategic approach be to destroy hunger, or to rein in our expectations? We go to business school and we're told, think big, think more, ask more, don't be satisfied, stay hungry, stay fearful. We have valorized hunger in our culture. Not contentment.

Hunger makes us innovate no doubt. Hunger made us design planes and ships and spacecraft. Contentment would stop humans from travelling, exploring, holidaying. The very same imagination that creates abundance also creates boredom and frustration. For, in the imaginary world, nothing is enough. Nothing is good enough. The craving for more makes us constantly feel deprived even when successful. We feel poor in the midst of riches. The mind experiences scarcity despite material abundance. Imagination destroys contentment.

Contentment is seen as anti-capitalist, anti-entrepreneurial. We are encouraged to be dissatisfied in schools today. Dissatisfaction is seen as a drive needed for growth and development and progress. And so we end up being neither grateful nor generous. We refuse to accept reality and live in imaginary worlds of 'what if'. We don't appreciate the hospital when we are in pain because we expect it to be there, available to us. We feel we are entitled to it – because we worked hard, were good, we paid taxes, followed laws, and kept our part of the social contract.

We don't see the small solutions to life's problems as awesome. A toilet appearing magically when the bladder is bursting. A police van appearing when we feel we are being stalked. In striving to create predictability in life, we forget that the thrill of life, its joys and its tragedies, lies in its unpredictability.

In the Ramayana, Ram has two forms. One is called Ayodhya Ram, the other is Aranya Ram.

Where does hopelessness come from?

Ayodhya Ram (Ram, the king of Ayodhya) has all the luxuries and privileges of the elite, and Aranya Ram (Ram of the forest) is where he has none of it. The poets say that Ram's personality doesn't go through any change. He is tranquil in the city and is tranquil in the forest. His tranquillity is only disturbed when Sita is taken away from him. His loss of tranquillity comes from his fear for Sita and not from the cruelty of life or unfairness of the world. He wants to save Sita; he does not have any desire to change the world.

This idea of contentment – that my life is not a function of my privilege – is a very important idea in the Ramayana. Ram is happy with whatever he has. But he is not insecure about losing it. He is aware that what he has can go away in a split second – because of a jealous Kaikeyi or a vengeful Ravana. His abundance exists in the midst of other people's scarcity.

None can create a world where one exists without the other. And so we have to accept that things will not always go our way. We cannot control things entirely. We cannot make life predictable. We can create opportunities and allies, but there will always be threats and rivals.

In the Mahabharata, during their forest exile, Krishna pays the Pandavas a visit. A distraught Draupadi is unable to offer him a decent meal. She presents an empty bowl to Krishna to demonstrate how destitute she, who was once a queen, is. Krishna notices a grain of rice and eats it. He focuses on what is present, not what is absent. He focuses on abundance, not scarcity.

Abundance happens when we focus on what we have. Scarcity happens when we focus on what we do not have. In abundance, we enjoy the fact that we got a hospital bed. In scarcity, we moan the fact that the hospital bed is in a general ward.

A friend of mine had a daughter when he was almost 50. And he said, 'Devdutt, I want to give her all the happiness in the world, I want to give all the wonders of life to her.' I frowned. He asked why. I said, 'Because you are teaching her an unrealistic thing. You are not preparing her for a world where she may not get what she desires. If you satisfy all her desires, she will assume that the whole world, not just you, will satisfy her desires all the time. You're not preparing her for disappointment and heartbreak, which is part of life. Life is scarcity too.'

A crisis is a reminder of the myth of abundance. It is a reminder that abundance is neither permanent nor universal. Just as our imagination enables us to visualize worlds of greater abundance and greater scarcity, this very same imagination can rescue us in a moment of crisis, or create a crisis where there is none.

Just as the hope of winning draws us repeatedly to a gambling match, the hope of things getting better saves us from feeling miserable. We know that things can change at any corner. That makes us vigilant to reality. That also creates imaginary scenarios that eclipse our well-being with anxiety.

Fatalism as strategy

One of the best ways to find calmness and strength is by telling ourselves the crisis was supposed to happen. It calms us down immediately. Fatalism is a coping response, it's not a truth. If we're successful, it humbles us. If not, it reduces disappointment. This is the power of subjectivity. We can tell our mind to be positive or negative.

To accept things as they are is not always the healthiest approach in every situation. We can be deterministic in moments of abundance, but **in moments of scarcity, we have to reorient ourselves.** These are the various tools that we have to cope with the crisis. The question is, how do we go back to the balanced, tranquil state in the middle of a war, in the middle of a crime, in the middle of a flood? How do we do that? And I think these are questions to ask. We have limited control over the objective world – nature and culture. We can influence it to a degree. But human impact on nature and culture is collective. Individually, we have more control on our mind – the brahmanda.

The West is obsessed with determinism, that we can shape the world, make it a better world with better technology or better tools. We know what has happened when we have tried to change the world. It has led to colonialism, imperialism, destruction of ecosystems, social inequality.

But we persist in the elusive goal of a world where there will be equal opportunities for all. And this approach – that we can change the world, make it a better place when there is no historical evidence of such transformations – is itself an absurd idea. But the West does not want to confront it. Instead, it mocks fatalism as laziness and valorizes revolution.

Ram, the ideal man, accepts his exile but his brother doesn't. Is Ram fatalistic or realistic? Is Lakshman, his brother, more action-driven, a seeker of justice, who does not accept his fate? In Indian metaphysics, karma is the way the world functions, an outcome of collective action while kama is our personal desire, of how the world should be. And there will always be conflict between the two. The question is, how do we manage this?

Are we lazy when we think like Ram, or merely practical, where we do not want to blame anyone? **Are we more heroic when we** hold someone responsible and seek justice? The storyteller is trying to create a narrative of conflict by creating these two characters who approach life differently. He knows the normal response and therefore he creates a Lakshman who represents such an emotion, and then there is a refined response because our journey is to refine our lives. Lakshman is Nara, the human, who gets stressed in crisis. Ram is Narayana, the divine potential located within man, who does not get stressed in crisis.

One of the oldest existing temples in India is a fifth century temple in Deogarh, Uttar Pradesh. Carved on its structure is a beautiful image of two people talking. Look carefully and you will notice that one of them has two arms and the other has four arms. One is divine and the other is not. One is the teacher, Narayana, and the other is the student, Nara. So the journey from human to divine, Nara to Narayana, is represented visually by these four arms. You immediately know visually that one is supernatural. And what do they mean by supernatural?

For the West, supernatural God is someone who is very powerful. And it is a power that manifests in the social world. He solves social problems, through laws and judgement. It is not psychological at all. The supernatural in India, however, is subjective, psychological, involving refinement. Narayana is not about social transformation; it is about psychological transformation. And that's the fundamental difference.

Western myths want to change the objective world; it is about the good life and revolution. Indian myths are about refining oneself, so we respond to a crisis with grace. We enjoy the opportunities, we rise up to challenges, but do not feel the need to classify people as heroes, victims, and villains. For Ram, there is no villain in his story. Just people responding to a crisis, doing foolish things when their ego is hurt. For Lakshman, the world is full of mean and horrible people like Kaikeyi, like Ravana.

Folk mythology in India is full of heroes who rise against tyrants, who save cows from thieves and tigers. They are called vir and worshipped outside villages. Megaliths and hero-stones are raised in their honour.

The vir defeats external enemies – the thief, the tyrant, the villain, the invader. But the one who refines the mind is called a mahavir, the great hero. The mahavir defeats his own mental knots: jealousy, anger, expectations, attachments, frustrations, greed, ambition.

Western mythology loves the vir who gives hope and takes away hopelessness. The Indian worldview too celebrates the vir. But it prefers the mahavir who looks at life and knows the power of the mind to turn challenges into opportunities, find hope in hopelessness, be content in scarcity, and calm in crisis.

4

How do we handle a crisis?

We lose hope when the world seems bereft of opportunities. Or when we feel we have no strength to fight threats. In regular times, we feel there is an opportunity, there is support, we can reach out to family, friends, or state institutions.

But in a crisis, there is no one we feel we can turn to. All doors are shut. We feel helpless. Terrified. Alone. Like Sunahashepa at the sacrificial altar, like Sita alone in Lanka, like Draupadi dragged by the hair, like the Pandavas wandering homeless in the forest, like Nala wanting to run away from Damayanti, like Uttara holding the body of her dead husband on the battlefield.

What do we do at the moment of a crisis? This chapter is about action, not analysis. It is about focusing on the moment rather than providing perspective. Unlike other chapters, this is highly prescriptive. How do we pull ourselves from the precipice? There are five steps.

- The first step is to use breath and body to calm the mind so that we can think and figure a way out of hopelessness. We will explore why even Krishna, in the Gita, recommends focusing on the breath.

- The second is to locate our emotions. Do we need to feel angry, disappointed, depressed and hurt? Or can we cast them away, at least temporarily? How do we do that?

- The third is analysis and action using various frameworks such as mantra–tantra–yantra and have–find–do–ask.

- The fourth step is to pay attention to those in-between spaces as we wait for things to change when boredom and restlessness strike and we panic.

- The fifth step is to shift the focus on to others. Managing our personal hopelessness is different from dealing with those around us who look to us for hope. How can we be of assistance to a friend who is low, lost, seeking answers, maybe even suicidal?

The point of this chapter is to find ways by which we can drag ourselves, and those around us, out of the black hole and find the sun.

Step 1: Deal with the panic

When threatened, our body is conditioned to go into panic mode. It is called the stress response. The blood moves to the muscles – that is why our skin pales and the heart beats faster. It is an animal response to a crisis, designed by nature, to help us run away from threats like forest fires or predators. Or to fight. It is called the fight-or-flight response, very visible in animals. This stress or panic is useful when you are under immediate physical threat. But not in other situations of fear. Not when you have lost a job, or a loved one, or are desperately seeking a friend or a doctor. When the threat is not immediate, you don't need to panic. You need to relax, get rid of the stress so that you can think.

The way to do that is to **focus on your breath and your body.** Shvaas aur shareer, in Hindi. In the Bhagavad Gita, when Arjuna is having a nervous breakdown, Krishna speaks of pranayama: in chapter 4, verses 29 and 30, and chapter 5, verses 28 and 29, he talks about holding one's breath and releasing it. He talks of how this practice takes away hunger and fear, which prevent a person from thinking clearly.

In a crisis, our heart explodes, our brain feels numb. But the one function that never stops is our breath. As long as we are alive, we will breathe. As we fear the worst, we must take a minute to just feel our breath, remind ourselves that we are breathing, that we are alive.

I am not saying manipulate the breath. I am not talking of inhalation, exhalation, anything as such. Just be aware of your breath. And that will instantly centre you. There is something magical about the breath, which connects the external and the internal worlds and hence the sages talk about it. That is why even Krishna talks about it. Breathing helps us calm the mind and refocus our thoughts. Pay attention to your breath until it regularizes itself. Feel the air going in and out. Feel it along your nostrils and in your lungs. This simple technique is magical whenever you suspect you are going into a negative space.

Breathing has a double benefit, because breath itself is calming, and it also gives us a sense of achievement. I put an alarm on my mobile phone and say, okay, until the alarm doesn't ring, I will not keep a check on time. I sit still and observe my breath. Once my alarm goes off, I reset it. At some point, we completely lose touch with time and space and when the alarm rings, we get a sense of achievement, which triggers our mind to produce happy hormones.

Having focused on breath now we have to look at our body. The body needs to be hydrated. Drink a glass of water if you can. It really gives you a moment of pause. Often in dehydration our agitation is much higher. So hydrate the body, and if possible, eat something with it, a fruit or anything, preferably sweet. Give your body sugar. Don't think calories.

Go to the bathroom, pass urine, pass stools. I think these activities sound very mundane, but they help to centre us. A friend of mine recently lost her husband. And she told me, 'Devdutt, I couldn't do anything until I realized in the morning I had to go to the bathroom. And the simple act of walking towards it reminded me of my body, and my life ahead of me.'

In stress, our muscles contract and cramp. As if ready to flee, or fight, or freeze. We need to relax it. In tantra, there is a practice called nyasa, which means 'settling down'. You touch a part of the body, chant a mantra, and visualize a deity. It is designed to calm you down and make you aware of your body. The word tantra comes from 'tanu' or body.

The word pranayama comes from 'prana', which means breath as well as life. In shava-asana or the corpse-pose, the yoga teacher tells you to pay attention to every part of your body from the head to the toes in an unhurried manner over several minutes. Just put the timer on your phone and focus on each part of your body without bothering about time until the alarm rings.

All these processes – breath, hydration, awareness of the body – are aimed to remind you that you are alive, that you are not in immediate physical danger. That you have a future. That your body is healthy. And that should be the springboard of hope. You are now able to think and do things that will pull you out of negativity. Or else you will remain in the whirlpool of cramped muscles and choked breath, spiralling downwards.

Panic is not in the mind. It is in the body. Stress is not in the mind. It is in the body. Emotion is not in the mind. It is in the body. Our body is 'solidified mind', according to yoga and tantra. So we express our stress and emotion through the body. If you work on the body, you end up working on the mind.

Hence in yoga, much attention is given to breath and body, alongside meditation. We can work on streamlining thoughts through meditation, not the mind. To work on the mind, we have to work with the breath and body. First shvaas and shareer before anything else.

Step one. In a negative place, distract your mind. Look for solutions only when you're not in a negative place.

That is why Indian sages invented the nam-jaap, where people chant god's name – Ram or someone else's, the name is not important – repeatedly. You chant Ram's name 108 times for example. The reason behind the number is that it provides a goal. Shiva's dumroo is meant to rattle away negative emotion by entering our mind through its incessant beat. The chanting, like the dumroo, is a meaningless rhythmic activity. You make it meaningful by choosing the name of a deity that you are connected to. But it is really a repetitive, numbing activity, which is done to occupy your mind and push negative thoughts away.

This is the origin of kirtan. It is of course far more elaborate – during a kirtan people sit together and sing. It was traditionally done to deal with existential angst, ennui. Through this collective activity of singing, what is it that we try to do?

During depression, chemicals are released in the brain that make us sad, or more accurately, during depression our brain doesn't get the chemicals that make us happy. So we now need to create chemicals that make us happy.

Step 2: Deal with emotions

Now that my body has calmed down, and I'm breathing and feeling relaxed, reality stares right in the eye. I may have lost a job, have insufficient money, there could be death around me, or it could be the trolls creating a negative environment. Or it could be that I see the country going nowhere but downhill, as no longer safe for women, or as not providing hope for children. Be that as it may, the next approach should not be intellectual but emotional.

Think of what Krishna does in the Gita as he resolves Arjuna's crisis. The book begins with very intellectual answers or gyan yoga. But about halfway through, Krishna realizes the intellectual approach is not working, because Arjuna is completely distraught and frightened. That is when he addresses emotions – and speaks of faith or bhakti yoga. He speaks of trusting a higher force.

That is what a hug does to people. It makes them feel they are not alone. That there is love in the world.

In hopelessness, you are filled with fear and anger. These are emotions of Thanatos or death in Greek mythology. Counter it with love and affection and kindness, the emotions of Eros. **Think of people who love you, people who inspire you – parents, lovers, children, teachers, friends, family. Remind yourself of everyone who has been good and kind.** It may be a character in a novel. Even an animal or a plant. Someone who has comforted you. Let them dilute the negativity of emotions that spring in your heart.

Another way to get rid of tense negative emotions is to cry. It is okay to cry. Let the tears acknowledge your sense of hopelessness and helplessness. A good cry is energizing. It does not make you weak. It is not a cry for help or support. It is like vomiting out poisoned food. It is about cleansing your heart of all that troubles you, burdens you, builds within you and fetters you.

If you are with someone who is facing bad

news, touch the person. Don't worry about talking or saying something useful. Just be there. Doctors know that when a person is sick, you hold their hands, you massage their feet, you rub their hands, and make them feel that they are wanted, loved, and cared for and you communicate through touch.

You see that happening inside elevators and trains because that's a safe space for us and creating that safe space is important. You talk through your hand and you talk through your presence, and you talk, not necessarily with words but by doing things like giving people water. I think these things make a big difference. It centres people. It makes them focus.

Avoid argument at any costs, it doesn't help. It just creates negativity and panic. There is no need to think of immediate solutions, just pause for a moment. I think it is at this point that we talk about acceptance, about accepting a situation as is, not harping on as it should be.

Most importantly, park negative emotions. If you feel you need to feel angry and upset, write that down and revisit it later. Not at the moment of crisis. You need solutions to feel positive, not fuel for negativity. So **get out of negative emotions, at least temporarily. Grant yourself permission to visit them sometime later. Give those emotions an appointment: that you will feel anxiety at tea time or after a walk. Not now.** Thus you distance yourself from negativity, without rejecting it outright.

Step 3: Deal with the tasks

Once you are ready to think, focus on the matter at hand. There are many frameworks to use. I will discuss three of them.

The first is survival-success. Is your survival at stake or is your success being challenged? Where is the stress coming from? Is your life in danger? Do you not have food to eat, money to pay the bills? Or is your hopelessness coming from a vision of a bleak future where you may not have the kind of opportunities, status, or lifestyle you hoped for?

Survival-related issues are to be dealt with immediately. They are more physical. Success-related issues can be handled gradually. They are more psychological. For example, the Pandavas lose their kingdom and are banished to the forest. The immediate issue for them is finding food in the forest to eat. The long-term issue is getting their kingdom back, if Kauravas refuse to return it after the stipulated time. It is the same in the Ramayana. When Ram is exiled, he focuses on their survival, not on their return. We need to focus on the present, rather than let the future eclipse our mood today. A lot of things change between today and tomorrow.

The second framework is: have-find-do. Make a list of what you have. Then you will be able to figure out what you need. That leads you to a list of what you have to do, the list of tasks. So, you don't have a job. Does that mean you are going to starve immediately? Or that you have some things to take you through for a few days?

Make a list of what you have. Restrict it not just to the material things but also to the privileges you have – friends, support network, skills you possess.

This leads you to the task of finding the things you need to live a better life. It leads you to the to-do list that will help you find them. It could be looking for jobs in online job portals, asking friends, preparing résumés. It could mean attending interviews.

When things don't work out, move to the next task. Notice: there is no scope for 'thinking' in this framework. The point of finding and doing is to remove the thinking part once the list is done, or else negativity seeps in.

Sometimes when the tasks get overwhelming, I say to myself, 'I will do what I can do, and I will not do what I cannot do.' A simple reminder that helps me through the day. And at the end of the day, I focus on what I have done, not what I have not done, and I am usually amazed with what I have achieved.

I make a checklist of what I need to do the next day, but then I make a checklist of what I have done today. I end with achievements, because the sense of triumph makes me feel good – it helps me sleep better. A list of what needs to be done later or what still needs to be accomplished just creates anxiety and comes in the way of a good sleep.

In my to-do list, I always add joyful things – meeting positive people, enjoying my coffee, giving myself a break or a snack. Small joys of life. Let us not forget, to bring a smile on Draupadi's face during the exile, Bhima brought her lotus flowers. The little gestures matter.

The third framework that I use is mantra-tantra-yantra. Mantra deals with mental issues. Tantra deals with physical issues. Yantra, with technological issues. Let me explain with an example. Recently my driver was taking a turn and a speeding bike came from the wrong side of the road and hit the car. My driver called me up immediately. I was filled with dread. Had someone died? What would be the cost of repairing the car? Was my driver safe? Was he being threatened?

I used the mantra-tantra-yantra framework. First I thought of the body (tantra). Did someone die? He said, no. Had anyone been hurt? He said no. Then I focused on the mind (mantra). I focused on calming my driver down.

I told him to calm the biker. Accidents happen. And everyone blames the other.

Only the parties involved know the truth, but the only way to prove it is through a reliable third-party witness or better still a camera. Finally, I focused on the technology (yantra): the damage to the car, the bike, the financial implications, insurance, if the police needed to be called since law is also 'social technology' located outside the body and the mind.

What did Ram do on his first day in the forest? I always ask this question in my workshops with children. The kids respond saying Ram would have gathered berries and fruits because he would have to eat. Because no matter what you may be going through, every few hours, your stomach will growl and you have to eat, and you have to drink. And I think that's a very practical way of looking at things.

Frameworks help us make a list of things. I am a major list-maker; I think that organizes the mind. You don't have to stick to the list. I keep tearing old lists and making new ones. Because it gives me a sense of purpose. What should you make a list of? Again, it comes down to what your primal needs are. Your primal needs are hunger and fear, and they have to be managed, of them, hunger being the more important.

Step 4: Deal with the waiting

Between overcoming anxiety and working on the solution, there are long hours of waiting. We often ignore this reality. That is when I think it is time to do mundane, boring, meaningless, but practical tasks. It could be things like tidying the room, taking a bath, choosing and wearing clean clothes. Organize the space around you, eat something, drink something, exercise if you can, have a meal. If possible, lie down, take a nap.

Mundane chores for me are very useful. Don't watch movies unless you really need to do something, because movies can trigger ideas as can books. Traditionally you were told to listen to bhajans and kirtans during a difficult time. Music plays a very powerful role in calming some people, but music can also agitate depending on what you want to hear. Hear something positive, uplifting, or spiritual. Avoid introspective lyrics.

Sita is kept in the Ashoka Vatika in Lanka. The irony is, she's in this unhappy place, but it's called Ashoka Vatika, the garden of joy or the garden without sorrow. It's a very interesting name used by Valmiki – after all Sita has been captured, this garden of joy is her prison. She is supposed to have invented a game like solitaire at this time. It's called Sita pandi in South India. She invented the game using the seeds of a fruit to entertain herself while she was stuck.

What do we do when we are bored? Our mind loves getting excited so much that when we get bored, we want new excitement. We open the fridge for food, we consume alcohol, watch movies, and we train our minds to get hyper-excited with all wasteful and negative things.

But **during a crisis, when we're lying in bed at the end of the day, can we do something positive instead?** We can count, we count sheep, we can count the names of god. We can make checklists. How many clothes do I have? How many undergarments do I have? How many curtains do I have? How many bricks are there on this wall? How many ants can I see? The brain seems to respond to these simple counting games.

Which is perhaps why Sita invented her game – to distract herself from negative thoughts. And in the end, the hope is these exercises will still the mind and lead you to sleep. I think sleep is a very powerful remedy for people. This is the only time when I advise people to take medication on doctor's advice that helps them sleep. Today there are a lot of home remedies to help with this too.

The point is, we don't want your mind to think while waiting, we want to prevent it from wandering into a negative space. So even if you can't sleep, just shut your eyes and maybe put an eye mask. Surround yourself with good smells, washed sheets, be in a neat and clean room. **The most important thing is not to think until it is time for the next task.**

Step 5: Deal with others

When you help a friend or family member deal with a tragedy, you should first check if you are dealing with clinical or non-clinical depression. If it is the former, the person needs the assistance of experts – a doctor, a therapist, a physiotherapist. The person's state of mind needs specialized care and you can't do it on your own.

But if it is a transient mood thing, just be around them, do your stuff and nudge them gently within your capacity. As I said, the coping steps should move from the breath, the body, the emotion, the mind, to the tasks, and to gradually socializing with all.

Be there to help the depressed come out of the dark cave towards the light very gently. **But remember, you are not there to direct them, you are not there to control them. It's their battle. Don't indulge the negativities, don't fight them.** People want you to agree with them. So agree with them. It feels good when you agree with even stupid ideas, and then gently nudge them away from those ideas.

One technique that I have found very useful is that, when someone says something negative, dilute it. Don't fight it. So if they're focused on something negative, establish a perspective whereby the negativity is completely diluted. This is a very Indian approach. If there are too many spices, you don't put the counter spice. You just put more water and dilute the taste or add a potato, which will absorb everything. I think that's an important technique to use if you see someone getting too negative.

It's a very clever game, because they will like you if you agree with them, and dislike you if you don't. And you have to play this game in your way, which is dilute their claims and tell the big story where their agreement feels silly even to themselves.

I'll give you an example. Someone says the world is coming to an end, all these politicians are ruining the world. Now if you say that's not true, they will get very upset with you and so you agree with them and you say but in life, politicians come and go and the sun rises whether they are there or not.

You have now diluted the conversation, and I've seen people not know what to say in response to such a statement. It's the ultimate truism, the big picture. And with that, the pettiness of that moment is wiped out. If they are bitchy about a mother-in-law or a daughter-in-law, you have to agree with them first. Then talk of the grand picture, like how we will all grow old and bowel movements will become more important than kitchen battles. In this large picture, their thoughts will seem petty and silly. Or remind them of the times when they were more generous and kinder, and wiser and smarter.

I think **we must remember that in caring for others, we are at the risk of controlling them.** Of course to help, sometimes, we have to discipline the other because they can't do it themselves. They are like children in the moment of crisis. And in the way we discipline children, we must make them eat, go to the toilet, sleep. But we must keep reminding ourselves that in the process we may end up giving ourselves a control high. Their failures become our failures, and their successes, our successes. We indulge our ego, through them.

It is our mind playing this game with us, we start becoming possessive of who we take care of. We expect them to do exactly what we tell them to do, we love them for being obedient and we get sucked into the game, forgetting it is their battle not ours. We are there to enable, enrich and empower, and we may fail, and it's okay. It's okay to fail.

I once had a neighbour, a 90-year-old man, and he lived with his daughter who was in her 60s. He would say to her, 'I want to eat sweets,' and she would say 'no'. And they would have huge fights and he would sulk, and she would sulk. I reminded her that he was 90. 'What's wrong with you? Give him what he wants to eat.' She said, 'No, he will be ill.' I said, 'Okay, he'll be ill, but he's old, he's ill already. Focus on his life, not on his death. Don't fight death and make his life bearable.'

We often forget what the goal is. The daughter's goal in the earlier example was to make sure her father approaches death as gracefully as possible. As I argued with her, I realized the old man had become the caregiver's purpose in life. If he died, she would be left with no purpose. She was fighting for her purpose. His staying alive was important for her. Without the daily chores, and the daily frustrations, she had nothing to do. Or so she thought.

As I write this book, I read a tweet about a 39-year-old man who had killed himself. He had lost his job during the second wave of COVID-19, fallen into depression, lost touch with everyone, and killed himself. This is not a stray incident. So many have taken this path during this difficult period. What do we do when we meet someone like that? A friend or family member maybe?

The first thing to consider in such a situation is whether the hopelessness being expressed is a medical issue that requires professional intervention. Great care is essential in handling depression. Pep talk or managing the thought process is not a solution for a person with clinical depression. The problem requires expert intervention.

If the one experiencing depression is you and it is chronic, if you feel that you are losing interest in the small pleasures of life too, like eating or going out or meeting friends, and do not feel like getting out of bed, I would urge you to see a doctor.

Remove the shame around depression. Remove the shame around mental illness. Think of it is as 'food poisoning of the brain'. We are shy to talk about diarrhoea and gas issues, but not ashamed. We should extend this to mental ailments. When we remove shame around mental issues, more people will come forward and seek help.

Young people experiment with drugs – it can destroy lives. Rather than getting moralistic about it, we have to discuss it and understand where the urge to experiment comes from. Is it experiment or habit? Is it pleasure or compulsion? These conversations generate trust and then our advice has a greater chance of being effective.

Meeting depressed people can be exhausting. If we cannot get a grip over the situation, we must avoid such encounters. But if we can handle it, we must help them. When we feel hopeless and useless and helpless and down, we turn into black holes. By turning into black holes, I feel we suck the energy from everyone around us, spreading negativity without meaning to. When you meet such 'black hole' people, you also go back home feeling depressed, because it's contagious. Negative energy is contagious. It's a reality we have to admit.

Earlier in the book, I've spoken of Nala Damayanti and Nala's story is this 39-year-old man's story. He loses his kingship and everything he tries fails, and he feels hopeless and he feels judged by everyone around him. He feels small. His self-image and self-worth take a horrible beating and he withdraws from the world. In the man's case, he didn't want to feel anything, so he kills himself.

In Nala's case, he disappears. We are told that he uses a magic potion and destroys his looks so that nobody recognizes him. He looks old and withered and bent. He joins as a servant in a king's palace and becomes a cook. He lives his life in complete isolation and solitude. That's what many people do, they withdraw from the public eye.

What brings Nala out of his shell finally is Damayanti, who believes in him, who clings to him saying we'll manage. It's not about happily ever after. She's there for Nala but also to remind him that he is merely thinking of himself while there are people around him who need him to be their sun.

Everybody around you is a black hole, and nobody energizes you. You probably perceive yourself as the black hole. No one is looking in my direction, there's no lotus blooming because of me, there is no flower blooming because of me. There is no bird chirping because of me, there's only darkness.

Because I'm the black hole, I just consume, consume, and consume, and I do not bring value to anybody, therefore I feel valueless. And when I feel valueless, I also feel helpless. And that is where hopelessness comes in.

But have you realized that you energize people around you, somebody at least, and they need you to survive? And your presence alone is enough to give them energy. The sun doesn't do anything for plants, but the presence of the radiant sun helps plants grow. When we are feeling very hopeless we forget that we always bring value to the people around us.

If your friend or family is low, it is important for you to be the sun and to remind them that they are the sun too. They need to be reminded that as the sun, you're giving them energy. That's the reason they've come to you. But you have to make them realize that they too play the sun to many people. We give energy to someone or the other.

We have to surround ourselves with people who energize us, and we should energize other people. Talk about the good times, admire each other's strengths and achievements, however small they may seem, share what inspired you about them.

When you watch wartime movies, you will see a man singing or a man playing the flute or someone touching someone's hand. What do such characters represent? In those contexts, they transform into the sun that radiates energy and life, renewing others, so that flowers can bloom, birds can sing.

It is important that you are surrounded by people who are generous. Do we have a Damayanti in our lives? Damayanti could be a mother, a father, a friend, a sibling, or anyone – people who hold on to you and remind you that you are their sun.

Not everybody will be able to do that, some people die by suicide. I don't see suicide as failure. Some people couldn't make it, and it is okay. It's not a criminal act. It's not a terrible act. But the person could have lived a rich life, and that's a tragedy. A possibility was lost – that is the tragedy and not the fact that the person couldn't take it any more and decided to end his or her life. I feel sad for the man I read about on Twitter, but I would not like to judge him.

5

How do we become
more resilient?

Often after attending a funeral people get depressed and philosophical and wonder if there is any point in life. They wish to give up everything. This state is called smashan vairagya, a loss of interest in life triggered by a visit to the cremation grounds. People are overwhelmed by hopelessness and meaninglessness at the sight of death. To counter this, a feast is organized shortly after the cremation. You eat, and with your stomach full, you forget the negative thoughts and move on.

When we are in the middle of a crisis, we feel the world is collapsing and nothing's worth it. But the moment life starts getting better, when spring returns, we think of summer and look forward to the beach, holidays, and parties.

We may forget the crisis entirely and return to our old ways. But the crisis will return, in one form or the other. We will soon forget COVID-19, as people forgot the Partition, and the world wars despite large billboards asking us to 'Never Forget'. Humans forget. Memory is too burdensome. But is that wise?

Jain mythology tells us that time moves like a serpent, undulating upwards towards good times and downwards towards bad times. This happens with unfailing regularity. In the Jain worldview, the seeds of good times are sown in bad times and vice versa. In other words, a crisis in one form or the other will always recur in life. There is little escape, no matter what society promises us. It, therefore, makes sense to be resilient to the passage of time rather than feel fragile and undone when life takes a turn for the worse. We must prepare ourselves for the next crisis.

Through the book, we have made a journey from acknowledging feelings of hopelessness, thinking about the origins of hope as well as hopelessness, to finding ways to manage a crisis.

In this chapter, I recommend seven key ways to build resilience.

How do we become more resilient?

- Retrain your gaze using the concept of 'darshan' and realize how the way we see creates fragility or resilience.
- Repurpose storytelling so that stories are not deployed to shut out reality with false promises as a way of protecting children. Instead, narrate stories that encourage resilience in the toughest of times.
- Explore the truth of the forest, where things can go wrong any time, for anyone, rich or poor, mighty or meek, for no fault of theirs.
- Through the assortment of stories available from around the world, learn to appreciate the diversity and dynamism of life.
- End the saviour complex that plagues the Western (and hence modern global) narratives. It makes us want to scold people who do not behave as per our expectations.
- Admit your mortality. Discuss death and prepare for the end of life.
- Contemplate gratitude and generosity. Being grateful for the help received is good but being generous in helping others is better, for the latter creates opportunities, which brings hope.

Retrain your gaze

Ram is devastated when Sita is abducted. All he knows is that someone has taken her in the southern direction. He walks in that direction consumed by a feeling of dread, not eating, not sleeping, when he encounters a tribal woman, Sabari. Sabari offers him some berries to eat. Ram has not eaten in days, so he accepts her invitation. Sabari takes a bite of each berry before offering it to Ram.

Ram accepts the 'jhoota' or soiled berries with grace. But Lakshman is livid and accuses Sabari of lacking manners. Ram tells Lakshman, 'You have sight but no insight. You lack darshan. You see a woman without manners. She has no understanding of royal manners as she has lived in the forest all her life unlike you who is judging her by the standards of the palace. I see a kind and generous woman trying to give me the sweetest of berries.'

In this story, Lakshman is angry with the world for not matching up to his standards, while Ram understands the world for what it is. Lakshman creates a crisis, a subjective crisis, based on his values and rules and expectations. Lakshman behaves like the Pea Princess or Rajkumari Matari. Ram is like the Flame Princess or Rajkumari Jwala. These two princesses are metaphors of how we see the world, how we execute darshan.

I have deliberately used feminine metaphors and masculine characters to explain this point as I want to teach you and your children to focus on the idea, not the gender. Ideas have no gender.

Rajkumari Matari cannot sleep on her bed even if there is one little pea under a dozen mattresses. Rajkumari Jwala, on the other hand, can walk through fire without being singed. The fundamental difference between the two is that Pea Princess feels that the world owes her comfort, like Lakshman in this story, while Flame Princess finds comfort in every circumstance, like Ram in this story. Rajkumari Matari is poor even in abundance, while Rajkumari Jwala finds prosperity even in scarcity. The two see the world differently and so respond to the objective reality very differently.

Rajkumari Matari sees a world full of heroes who rescue her and villains who make life tough for her. She loves those who create Swarga for her and hates those who create Naraka. Rajkumari Jwala sees the world full of potential. With people around her, she can create Swarga and avoid Naraka.

In other words, power rests outside for Rajkumari Matari, making her a helpless damsel who fears monsters and needs saviours. For Rajkumari Jwala, power rests inside, within her. She realizes that there is a monster and a saviour within all of us, and we have to navigate through this world, evoking the best in everyone we encounter. Pea Princess seeks hope and fears hopelessness. Flame Princess carries hope wherever she goes.

Rajkumari Jwala is resilient. And her resilience comes from her darshan. She recognizes the existence of three worlds: nature (prakriti), culture (sanskriti) and imagination (brahmanda). Nature is the world of hunger and fear, common to all humanity. Culture is a world of rules and values, different for different communities.

Brahmanda is personal. There is only one nature. There are many cultures. And there are as many brahmandas as there are people. Everyone we encounter sees the world differently, shaped by their personal experiences and personal education within a given culture.

Rajkumari Matari is busy judging the world as good or bad, right and wrong. She is anchored in her culture and so expects the world to behave according to a set of laws, ethics, and morality that makes sense to her. Rajkumari Jwala recognizes the hungry and frightened beast in everyone, domesticated by culture, but yearning for resources, power, and meaning. She navigates and negotiates her way through these beasts, making allies, avoiding rivals, collaborating rather than competing.

When people are rude, when help is not forthcoming, when opportunities are scarce, when things appear bleak, Rajkumari Matari feels sorry for herself and finds people to blame. Rajkumari Jwala, on the other hand, sees this as part of life – a calamity like a forest fire where tigers and deer run together to avoid the flames, a disaster that occurs when demand outstrips supply, when patience is tested, and when even basic human decency is forgotten by the frightened and the insecure. Rajkumari Matari seeks angels who will rescue her from demons. Rajkumari Jwala becomes the bodhisattva who gives up all expectations and is generous with compassion.

We see patients fighting with doctors, nurses being rude to caregivers. In darshan, we see the insecurity of all living organisms and their perception of themselves. **What if we step out of the 'good–bad framework' and step into the 'hunger–fear framework'? Could this scene also be telling another story? That insecurity makes people bark at each other like hungry dogs fighting over meat.**

The fighting doctors, nurses and patients then appear not as heroes, villains, or victims, but as scared human beings, confused about their rights and roles and responsibilities, unable to be grateful and generous. Our own darshan shifts from being judgemental to being compassionate. Instead of taking sides, we work to resolve the situation. We stop being Pea Princess and become Flame Princess, bringing light into dark situations.

Darshan is also about recognizing that nothing lasts forever. In nature, the flood and forest fire eventually come to an end. In culture, rules and values keep changing. People's emotions keep changing. Nothing is static. A crisis comes and goes.

In a crisis, the world looks terrifying and everything around seems to collapse, making us very scared. But civilizations go through cycles, cultures go through cycles, fortunes go through cycles, families go through cycles. Animals go back to living as before when a crisis ends, but we as humans have the option to stay fragile or be resilient.

Change your stories

Krishna helps the Pandavas but ends up being cursed by the mother of the Kauravas. Why does that happen? Ram liberates Sita from Ravana but ends up abandoning her. Is that a problem with our story, or our expectations of how stories have to end? Are these stories telling us a truth we do not want to confront, that **bad things can happen to good people, that good efforts need not guarantee good results? That life is unpredictable, uncertain?**

Our education has not prepared us for a tough life, a difficult life. We try to ban bullying rather than enabling children to stand up to bullies. We valorize rule-following but do not prepare the children for a world where people may not always play by the rules or even agree with them. We tell children that a good life is created by material opportunities when, in fact, it is created through an engagement with the world as it keeps transforming. We try to establish Swarga, full of opportunities, but ignore Naraka, full of threats that the children may have to deal with again and again in future.

School life should be like army training. It doesn't mean there is going to be a war, but the soldier must be trained to prepare for any eventuality. Most soldiers are trained to fight external enemies but end up working to save lives internally during calamities and disasters. When there is a crisis, will our children know how to handle it? Do schools teach children to panic or manage panic? Do schools prepare children to be damsels in distress or guardian angels? The secret of education lies in the stories we tell our children, not just in the skills they gain. Stories shape darshan, teach them how to interpret the world, how to respond to a situation.

For centuries, we told stories, performed rituals and created symbols to cope with a very tough life. Primitive humans did not have claws, fangs, feathers, or scales. They could not fly or swim, but they had to survive.

Imagine hunter-gatherers living in caves, not knowing who may attack them from which corner. It could be bears, wolves, hyenas, tigers, lions, snakes, or scorpions. Sharp thorns of trees or sharp rocks on the floor. Thunder, rain, or flood. Our earliest ancestors lived in a state of absolute terror and all those memories are in our brains. They lived in a world of scarcity and crises, in Naraka, and yearned for the abundance of Swarga.

Humanity has had excess resources for barely 10,000 years, thanks to the agricultural revolution, but our brain has memories of the times long before. In our survival journeys, we have seen our friends die in front of us, we have seen families being ripped apart by typhoons and starvation and epidemics and drought, and all those memories, all those cultural memories are in our stories and rituals.

But we don't see stories, symbols, and rituals as sources of ancient primal knowledge. We see them as myths, as fiction because they use fantastic elements. The fantasies in these tales serve as metaphors, demonstrating that our ancestors tried to communicate complex ideas that defied the literal.

We are not born with ideas of hope and hopelessness. As children, we are helpless. We are frightened and hungry, and somebody takes care of us. We have someone taking care of us through our growing years. It takes a long time for human children to learn to survive on their own. They grow up hearing the stories of their elders and are told what to expect in the world.

How do we become more resilient?

One way to make our children strong mentally as they slowly move towards physical independence is by telling them stories that deal with danger, injustice, cruelty, and complications. Stories can breed fragility or resilience. Stories shape the lens through which we make sense of the world. These stories help us to experience difficult emotions through their characters and their life circumstances. It's a safe space. By immersing ourselves in these stories, we come out stronger. We are prepared for the battle of life.

But in modern times, we wish to protect children from such triggers. We don't want to stress them out. We don't want to train them for the battle of life. We take pride in parenting a Rajkumari Matari rather than a Rajkumari Jwala.

Take the Greek story of Hercules. A jealous god makes Hercules mad and in his madness, he kills his wife and children. To atone for these sins, he has to perform twelve tasks. But when we talk about the twelve tasks of Hercules, we speak of them as if they are heroic deeds, not part of his punishment. We focus on the many triumphs, rather than the shame and guilt and horror the precedes them. Hollywood retelling of Hercules makes him a happy family man. Why did Hollywood change the ancient story? For whose benefit?

Fairy tales often speak of helpless girls who are saved by handsome, brave boys and their union ushers in a happily-ever-after end. How does this story impact boys and girls? Are these to be seen as metaphors, beyond gender? Or are these to be taken literally? The stories tell us that women need men to save them. That marriage brings happiness forever. And that there is such a thing called 'true love'. Are we not conditioning our children for disappointment, depression, anxiety, and hopelessness when they encounter real life?

Imagine a child being told the famous Old Testament story of Sodom and Gomorrah where a city that did not obey God was destroyed by fire and brimstone. Islamic lore also refers to many cities wiped out by wind and storms and floods because they did not listen to God. It creates the idea that if you do not obey, you will be destroyed and punished.

These stories tell you that violence is acceptable if the opposing party doesn't agree or align with you. It makes for uncomfortable reading, and today's parents may find it too dark for their children. But these stories need to be told. Because such things do happen. Remember America bombed Hiroshima and Nagasaki with nuclear weapons as Japan refused to submit. If the child raises this moral dilemma, discuss it, don't justify it.

We must avoid the practice of establishing heroes, villains, and victims. Storytellers are not judges. They need children to figure out for themselves what is acceptable and what is not. What they will tolerate and what they will not.

In a safe place, which is the storytelling space, we are told about injustice and justice, good things and bad, about adventures and how things sometimes work out and at other times don't. Through them children are prepared for failure and success, they are told that when they're successful, they must check themselves from growing proud and arrogant. Many people would have contributed to your success. When you fail, don't feel down and out; people can survive. Accept that sometimes things just don't work out.

Remember the point is not to only tell the dark stories. You must tell the others too, stories where God is also loving and kind and gentle. Where cities are saved when people change. Prophet Jonas did not want to deliver bad news to the city of Ninevah saying that it would be destroyed as people were disobeying God's laws. He did not think his word would have any impact. He tried to run away. He even tried to kill himself. But he survived, underwater, in the belly of a whale. Finally, he went to Ninevah and told them God's message. To his surprise, the people changed their ways and God did not destroy the city. Jonas was angry as God had not kept his word. God said to him, people change, so decisions change. Nothing is static.

If we read the stories of prophets in the Bible, we see that there are always narratives and counter-narratives. Children will ask as you read them, 'What are you trying to say? Is God kind or cruel?' You must be clear that God can be both cruel and kind. Think situationally. Think contextually. Don't approach a story, a meeting, or any event with preconceived ideas.

After all, **life too is sometimes kind and sometimes cruel. Sometimes there is a happily-ever-after ending, but not always. And I think that's how storytelling has to be.** It has to bring alive the confusion of life, sometimes offering solutions or showing how things don't always work, how collaboration works in some cases and how competition works in others.

The point I am making is not just about how we tell stories to our children. By turning our lens on the way we tell stories, we are training ourselves to use this same lens in our own lives.

Tell children the story of the Ramayana and don't tell children that Ram is the hero or Ravana is the villain. Let the characters speak for themselves. Make the children question Ram's motives when he gives up his kingdom or chases the golden deer, or Ravana's motives when he abducts Sita or when he burns Hanuman's tale. Don't justify. Let children argue. Don't give conclusions.

We should not have an agenda when telling a story. We should not presuppose what the child is going to feel when you narrate the story because the child might surprise you. Just tell stories as they are, and of course, nudge the boundaries and see how they react to things that make them uncomfortable. Don't precondition the child to respond in a way you think a person should respond.

As they go to school and college, they have to deal with bullies, difficult teachers, demotivation, with jealous friends. Children can be extremely cruel, the playground can be extremely violent and, therefore, we have monsters and demons and ghouls in our stories.

We end up telling our children the story of Krishna growing up in Vrindavan. We're obsessed about this cute little superhero child with his many triumphs. But there is nothing cute about the stories – they are rather violent. Take the example of Putana, who kills all the babies by feeding them milk from her breasts covered in poison. But baby Krishna sucks the poison from her breasts and kills her. Or take the whirlwind that tries to pick up Krishna and toss him to the ground. It is about to smash him to bits when Krishna makes himself so heavy that the whirlwind cannot carry him any more. Then there is the Shakata story, where a big, heavy wheel rolls down to crush the boy as he is lying on the ground. We celebrate the victories of Krishna. It makes children feel powerful, helps them overcome anxieties and fears.

But we also need them to reflect on why so many people are trying to hurt Krishna. Why are they sending Putana and Shakata against Krishna? And such questions on motivations will draw attention to King Kansa's insecurities. How, in our state of fear, we do foolish things. We hurt and bully people. There is nothing cute about killing demons. Violence is not cute. Violence may be necessary to defend but it hurts people. And people thus hurt hit back, creating a spiral of violence.

Krishna's stories end with the god killing his evil uncle Kansa who has been plotting to kill him through his childhood. But the story does not end there. We edit out the consequences of Krishna's actions. Kansa's father-in-law, Jarasandha, the powerful king of Magadh, attacks and burns down Krishna's city of Mathura.

Part of wanting a neat story, tightly wrapped in happily-ever-after endings, stems from our need for a clear right and wrong, good and evil. We tend to bring a judgement lens to view our stories today. Yet our myths cannot be approached with the lens of judgement, the attempt only warps the story completely. Because then you are constantly asking is Ram right, is Ravana right? Is Ram fair? Is Bali right, and is Sugriv right? Are the Kauravas right or the Pandavas? Why should there be one perspective through which the story is read?

What if I could change the way I thought about the story? What if I say, people went through challenges and they responded to them differently? For example, Surpanakha desired someone and had her face cut up and so she was very angry. I'm not saying Surpanakha was right, and I'm not saying Lakshman was wrong. I'm not using the right–wrong vocabulary.

I'm looking instead at the choices that they made. And the choices are emotional. She was full of desire, she was smitten by Ram's and Lakshman's beauty. We have established a judge everywhere – there is this man with a wig and black coat following every character. And there is a lady with a blindfold holding a scale behind. These are not Indian ideas.

In the court of law, both the accused and the defender swear by the Bhagavad Gita. And both imagine themselves as betrayed parties. If we don't teach our children about complications through stories, that there is necessarily no right or wrong and that things don't always end well for the 'good' guy, how do we prepare them for the difficulties ahead? As readers, we often identify with characters in a story. But what if in Red Riding Hood we are the wolf, not the preyed-upon little girl?

Never forget the forest

The forest has been an important theme in this book. It is the background in which all stories are told in our myths. The Ramayana is about Ram going to the forest and the Mahabharata is about the Pandavas going to the forest. It's woven here through the chapters but as we end this book, I want to talk a little about it and what it means.

The earliest Indian holy book is the Rigveda, which is full of hymns. The Samaveda, which comes next, is a collection of melodies for these hymns. But the melodies are classified in a very specific manner. There are songs to be sung in the forest. And there are songs that must be sung in the settlement. It is the first time you have had this division in India, between songs of the forest and songs of the settlement. Now, why do they make this division between the forest and the field?

The Yajurveda, which comes later, talks of how these hymns have to be applied to rituals. Most of the rituals dealt with are kingship, governance, and social structures. These are then elaborated in two books. One is called the Brahmana and the other is the Aranyaka. The Brahmanas are rituals performed in the settlement, which expand your mind and make you think big. The Aranyakas talk of the things that are done in secret, rituals that have to be done in the forest. Once again, you have this division between the settlement and the forest.

And when you read the Ramayana and the Mahabharata, you're constantly told about kings who were exiled to the forest. Ram goes to the forest, the Pandavas go to the forest, Nala and Damayanti lose their fortune and go to the forest, Sita is banished to the forest by her husband. So the forest is a recurring metaphor. Now, what is a forest? What does it mean?

A forest is a place where nobody is there for you. You have to take care of yourself. You are in a place where you never know who will attack you, where there is no legislative or judicial body, no police or army. You can't complain to anyone if a snake bites you or a scorpion stings you or a bird shits on you. Remember, there is no one trying to hurt you or spite you deliberately. Each is trying to survive in the forest. Violence is simply the consequence of the quest to survive. **The forest represents Sunahshepa's world.**

When nobody takes care of you, there is no choice but to fend for yourself. What turns the forest into civilization is the ability of humans to take care of each other. I think this is the idea from where the Ramayana and the Mahabharata emerged.

And that is why these stories give value to the forest. Krishna is in the forest, Madhuban, Vrindavan. Hanuman is in Kardalivan, Ganesha is in Ikshuvan. The forest is thus the uncultivated untamed wilderness – the central metaphor of Indian thought where divinity springs from and enables us to discover our humanity, giving us hope and making us givers of hope to others.

Yet I think the stories keep telling us that humans can transform the uncaring forest into a garden of hope and delight. In the forest, everyone thinks only for themselves. But humans have the power to bring hope wherever they go. That is the divine spark. That Sunahshepa is helpless indicates no one around him, individually or collectively, has discovered the human ability to care – then there is no hope. We are back in the forest, where we have to fend for ourselves.

Appreciate life's diversity and dynamic nature

Not all land is covered by forests. Not all forests are the same. The same forest has different kinds of animals and plants. Humans, however, prefer to breed one kind of plant or animal in their farms for their benefit. Thus, humans tend to take away diversity. We prefer the certainty and comfort of homogeneity. In experiencing one way of being, we ignore the others.

In Hindu mythology, there are different kinds of creatures, all children of Brahma: rakshasas who live in the forest, pretas who live in crematoriums, nagas and asuras who live under the earth, devas and gandharvas who live in the skies. In Norse mythology, we hear of dwarves, giants, elves, humans, different kinds of gods living in different worlds perched on the branches of a great cosmic tree. Islam refers to humans and djinns and angels who live in different planes of existence. These stories are meant to make us aware of the diversity and the many worlds that exist around us.

Nowadays, **we are conditioned to turn all differences into hierarchies.** Are dwarves better than giants? Are djinns evil and angels good? Are devas better than asuras? Who is the oppressor and who is the oppressed? This happens because we are conditioned to think in terms of homogeneity and equality. Difference terrifies us. If we have more than others, we are expected to feel guilty. If we have less than others, we are expected to feel angry. But life will always exhibit differences. Some people will have more strength and more opportunities than others. But that is okay. There is no need to feel hopeless and abandoned because we are in a different situation.

Just because you live a privileged life doesn't mean everyone lives a privileged life. Just because you have been abused as a child doesn't mean everyone has had a similar experience. Just because you have had a positive childhood doesn't mean it is true for all. Just because you suffered COVID-19, doesn't mean everyone did; and just because you did not suffer health or job issues because of COVID-19, it doesn't mean others too have a similar story. Diversity is a very important vision to have. Everyone has their own brahmanda, their own subjectivity, their own experiences, traumas, and triumphs.

All rich people do not live the same life. All poor people do not live the same life. Everyone does not experience poverty the same way. Some may have loving parents despite poverty. Likewise, someone raised in an affluent society may not have loving parents. There are many dimensions to life and, therefore, from a diversity lens, we need to appreciate that all things are not bad in underdeveloped economies and all things are not good in developed economies.

Yes, there are more opportunities in developed economies, but this is simply the material lens. There is more to life than that. You can have a loving family with or without material resources. Material abundance does not guarantee emotional comfort. You could end up with an awful neighbour or a terrible boss. Diversity is about recognizing these intersections.

Diversity is about outgrowing the need to pity and patronize, or to privilege one thing over another. It is about recognizing good things and bad things everywhere. A family from Mumbai moved to Toronto for a better life. They had a great house in a year's time. But then during winter, the son slipped and fell on ice and broke his ankle badly so badly that he will limp forever.

Should the family blame the limp on the migration? Meanwhile, a Catholic girl from Canada came through an exchange programme to Mumbai, fell in love with a local girl, and decided to stay in the Mumbai suburbs with her. When asked, she said she preferred the understanding family in India to the orthodox homophobic family back home. Different people thus find hope in different places, in different contexts.

Animals migrate to lands where there is more food. So do humans. We move to land with greater opportunities. But then we become part of that ecosystem. All is good as long as there is abundance. But when the economy collapses and there is scarcity, people start competing with each other for resources. New settlers demand the same rights as others and this creates conflict.

Globalization seemed like a good idea in good times; in the bad times of today, the world is turning towards nationalism. America has turned its back on Afghanistan to focus on domestic affairs. Britain does not want to collaborate with Europeans. Ideas like universalism and homogeneity are being rejected. We forget that when we 'include diversity', we have to give up our comfort zone. When different people enter our ecosystem, life will not be the same.

There are predators in the savanna, in the desert, in the sea, and in the tropics. There is no part of nature devoid of them. Diversity is about appreciating this reality of life: opportunities and threats are everywhere, depending on how you choose to adapt.

You can be a hopeless and helpless Rajkumari Matari in different geographies and in different histories. But Rajkumari Jwala is aware that one's stay in Swarga is not eternal. Nor in Naraka. With diversity comes dynamism. Things change one way or the other.

End the saviour complex

The world is a problem, it needs a solution, I am the solution. This way of looking at the world – highly popular, very hegemonic, very Western – needs to be challenged. The world is not a problem. It is what it is. It has always gone through all kinds of ups and downs. There are all kinds of people – greedy, jealous, nasty, and nice. We live in a diverse ecosystem.

One of the reasons social media tells you negative stories is because it creates an ecosystem for the saviours. It makes you look for angels or turn yourself into one. If you are continuously told the situation is bad, the politicians who offer a good life or a product that promises joy will have a greater chance of success.

Whether it is science, technology, the media, or a public discourse like the communist or capitalist, all promise that they are going to create a world where the current situation will not exist. You will never suffer job loss, you will never fall ill, you will never have cancer, you will never die, you will never have heartbreak.

How do you guarantee that? Can anyone guarantee that?

Egyptian mythology speaks of an eternal world without suffering – after you die. Zoroastrian, Christian, Islamic, and Chinese myths also speak of that eternal peaceful afterlife for the good. **Buddhist, Jain, and Hindu mythologies do not speak of eternal joyful afterlives, even for the good. They say, you will be reborn. And there are no guarantees. An avatar may help you but just once. You may be saved occasionally, but not always. You may be in a place to help people, but only sometimes. You can be hopeful most of the time, but not always. The valley of despair cannot be avoided but it is not forever.**

Since World War II, there has been a persistent discourse that nation-states pursuing the development agenda can provide all material opportunities to everyone. That all countries can be like the Scandinavian Nordic countries. That there is a Promised Land that awaits all – provided we follow a particular universal path. The idea that human society can create good times for all human beings is deeply problematic. It does not acknowledge diversity. You may want to save and solve, but not everyone wants to be saved, and not everybody wants your solution.

We must be careful of our own assumptions about life. Indigenous people were never poor people. Yet, by calling them underdeveloped and poor, we have imposed our own values on them. And in building schools and hospitals for them to help them, we have contributed towards destroying their culture and heritage, just like invaders and marauders. Tribal people transmitted knowledge their way using stories and rituals, which do not make it to modern schools.

Assume a tribal school ends up teaching a standard curriculum approved by the education boards Delhi in Hindi – ignoring tribal languages. Is that ethical? Is that moral? What is a school for us is not a school for others. Concepts like human rights tend to be universal and ignore local rules and values and customs and beliefs. The great Left–Right divide we see in our society is because we want everyone to be on the same page. In other words, we want a homogeneous way of thinking. That is anti-diversity. Saviours on the Left side of society value the future and hate the saviours on the Right, who value the past.

Talk about death

We need to get death out of the closet and discuss it. We feel talking about death is bad. But often, it is the way to enjoy life more. People don't write wills or discuss insurance policies or end-of-life care with their wives and children and leave them in crisis when death strikes. **If during the good times you don't talk about death, when will you talk about it? You don't talk about death when it happens. Because that's the time you want to focus on life. Remember this simple rule: in the good times, talk about preparing for death and in the bad times, talk about the wonders of life.** We have to spend at least some time of our lives talking about death from a practical as well as an emotional point of view.

I have gone to financial seminars where I've asked wealth planners how many of them have made a will. And only about 10 per cent of hands are raised. We don't want to talk about death. We don't talk about insurance. And that's not healthy.

A friend tripped and had a fatal fall in one of the Mumbai train stations. He was only fifty. The certainty of life just slipped away because of one error, one misstep in a place he frequented every day to catch a train. His mother was sixty-nine at the time. And she had to deal with it virtually by herself as her husband was bedridden. When I went to meet his mother, she was so upset that she couldn't recognize me.

I think we have to invest time talking about the bad part of life once in a while, though not every day. During Gudi Padwa, a festival in Maharashtra and the Deccan area, along with sweets, you will be given something bitter to eat like a neem leaf. This is to remind you that life is not all sweet. You need a little bit of bitterness in your life, just as you need some bitter foods in your diet.

When I visit people who have lost a loved one, I notice most do not know what to say. Usually, silence is good enough. Your presence makes those bereaved feel less alone. But eventually, they have to go on without the person who mattered a lot in their lives. The widow, the widower, the brother, the sister, the parent, the friend. The absence of those who we care about makes us feel alone and meaningless. People around us, those with whom we actively engage, bring meaning to our lives. When they go away, that meaning is shattered.

At that time, do we hope? How will things get better? The dead will not return. The living will not replace the dead. With time, the dead will be forgotten. With time, we will find ways to cope with the emptiness inside us: the void they left behind. When I meet people who have lost a loved one, I talk to them about the meaning the dead person gave them. It helps to heal.

Death will always be there in this world. But we don't ever talk about it. We talk about the expiry date of fruits, vegetables, software, but we never talk about our own ending. I think because we don't talk about it, when we encounter death, it comes as a rude shock.

And it usually happens with sudden death rather than a passing away after a prolonged illness. Because during a prolonged illness, you eventually wish for the person to die so that both the sufferer and the caregiver are liberated.

But when it is sudden death, you are not prepared, and it shakes you up. The ashrama system in Hinduism, which divides life into four stages, shapes our life and conversations. As children, we talk about school. When we graduate, we talk about jobs and marriage and starting a family. When we retire, we talk about post-retirement activities like going on pilgrimages, visiting relatives and family homes, going to satsangs of gurus. But when do we talk about death? Do we ever talk to our partners about dying? Do we ask, 'What will you do when I'm gone?' Failure to do talk about eventuality sows the seeds of hopelessness when death strikes.

Be grateful, be generous

Before I end, I would like to talk about what I hope for you. This is also my strongest recommendation for developing resilience. I hope you are surrounded by generous people because I think then many problems will be solved. Rather than wish for a land of opportunities, I would seek a place where I meet people who are generous and kind, who understand and are able to give and receive with grace. I would like you to be surrounded by many radiant suns who will nourish you. That's my great hope.

My favourite story of generosity is of Indradyumna who spent all his life gifting cows to people. Gifting cows or godaan is a metaphor for livelihood. I think three thousand years ago when we moved from a pastoral economy to an agricultural one, 'giving cows' was a poetic way of representing the 'creation of livelihood'.

Indradyumna donated many cows as gifts and, therefore, he was given a place in heaven. One day Indra comes to him and says, 'You have to leave heaven because nobody on earth remembers your good deeds. So you'll have to go back to earth and live a life and again do some good deeds if you wish to return.' Indradyumna says, 'I did a lot of good deeds, it's impossible that people have forgotten what I've done.' Indra then tells him, 'If you can find even one person who remembers one of your good deeds, an act of generosity, you can come back to heaven.' Indradyumna goes back to earth looking for someone who remembers him.

Nobody recognizes him because thousands of years have passed. Indradyumna keeps travelling. He asks the oldest man and the oldest man takes him to the oldest bird, and the oldest bird takes him to the oldest tiger, and they all say 'No, we don't remember you.' Finally, they go to the oldest turtle who says, 'Oh, I remember you. My grandfather used to talk about King Indradyumna, who built the lake in which he was born.'

Indradyumna says, 'But I don't remember ever building a lake.' The turtle says, 'Well, you did. Remember all the cows you gave as gifts. When they were being given away, the cows would kick and raise a cloud of dust as they walked out of the royal cowshed. The depression they created collected water. Over time, it became a pond, which became home to many animals including birds, fish, turtles, and frogs. My grandfather was one of those who was born in that pond. Everybody told the story of the great Indradyumna, who gave so many cows away and because of this act, a lake was formed in which thousands of creatures were born, including my grandfather. It was over a thousand years ago but I remember the story because I heard this as a child.'

Indradyumna returns to heaven having learnt a profound lesson. He realizes that good deeds are not simply what you have done. You may have done many good deeds that benefited a large number of people, but you may not be even aware of them. Everything is not within your conscious domain. But you need to have faith.

Hope is when there is opportunity. Opportunity emerges when people are generous. **When I talk about generosity, I'm talking about the ability to give without expecting something**

in return. Materialism is about constantly asking, 'What is in it for me?' while spirituality is about asking, 'Does it have to be about me?' The more we think only about ourselves, the more we create an ecosystem of hopelessness around us, where none can look at us in hope.

Rather than asking why we cannot see abundance wherever we go, can we ask why we do not create abundance wherever we go? Rather than asking others to provide us opportunities, can we ask why we do not create opportunities? If we find black holes everywhere, can we try and be the sun for those around us? If we find no hope around us, can we be the hope for those around us? We may not be able to give material opportunities to all, but surely we can always give an emotional boost wherever we go. Remember, human beings create hope. To validate our humanity, we must be the fountainheads of hope for others.

Let us be an Indradyumna who spent his life creating opportunities for people around him. Yes, he did it to attain paradise. At a time when he lost all hope of being remembered, a turtle recognized Indradyumna for a noble deed he had done. Without being aware, Indradyumna had created a pond of hope where turtles thrived long after he was gone.

juggernaut

THE APP FOR INDIAN READERS

Fresh, original books tailored for mobile and for India. Starting at ₹10.

juggernaut.in

CRAFTED FOR MOBILE READING

Thought you would never read a book on mobile? Let us prove you wrong.

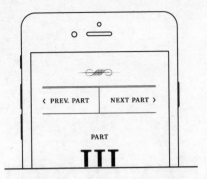

Beautiful Typography

The quality of print transferred
to your mobile. Forget ugly PDFs.

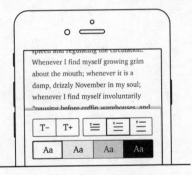

Customizable Reading

Read in the font size, spacing
and background of your liking.

AN EXTENSIVE LIBRARY

Including fresh, new, original Juggernaut books from the likes of Sunny Leone, Praveen Swami, Husain Haqqani, Umera Ahmed, Rujuta Diwekar and lots more. Plus, books from partner publishers and loads of free classics. Whichever genre you like, there's a book waiting for you.

DON'T JUST READ; INTERACT

We're changing the reading experience from passive to active.

Ask authors questions

Get all your answers from the horse's mouth.
Juggernaut authors actually reply to every
question they can.

Rate and review

Let everyone know of your favourite reads or
critique the finer points of a book – you will be
heard in a community of like-minded readers.

Gift books to friends

For a book-lover, there's no nicer gift than
a book personally picked. You can even
do it anonymously if you like.

Enjoy new book formats

Discover serials released in parts over
time, picture books including comics,
and story-bundles at discounted rates.
And coming soon, audiobooks.

LOWEST PRICES & ONE-TAP BUYING

Books start at ₹10 with regular discounts and free previews.

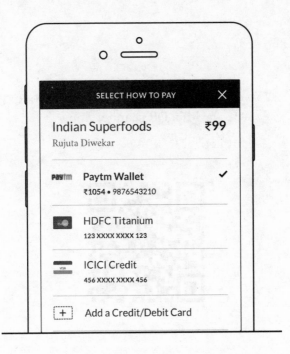

Paytm Wallet, Cards & Apple Payments

On Android, just add a Paytm Wallet once and buy any book with one tap. On iOS, pay with one tap with your iTunes-linked debit/credit card.

To download the app scan the QR Code
with a QR scanner app

For our complete catalogue, visit www.juggernaut.in
To submit your book, send a synopsis and two
sample chapters to books@juggernaut.in
For all other queries, write to contact@juggernaut.in